Assessment for Learning

Assessment for Learning

A Practical Approach for the Classroom

Eileen Dial

ROWMAN & LITTLEFIELD
Lanham • Boulder • New York • London

Published by Rowman & Littlefield
A wholly owned subsidiary of The Rowman & Littlefield Publishing Group, Inc.
4501 Forbes Boulevard, Suite 200, Lanham, Maryland 20706
www.rowman.com

Unit A, Whitacre Mews, 26-34 Stannary Street, London SE11 4AB

British Library Cataloguing in Publication Information Available

Library of Congress Cataloging-in-Publication Data

Name: Dial, Eileen, author.
Title: Assessment for learning : a practical approach for the classroom / Eileen Dial.
Description: Lanham, Maryland : Rowman & Littlefield Publishing Group, Inc., 2016. | Includes
      bibliographical references and index.
Identifiers: LCCN 2016002363| ISBN 9781475819694 (hardcover : alk. paper) | ISBN
      9781475819700 (pbk. : alk. paper)
Subjects: LCSH: Educational tests and measurements—United States. | Teaching—United States.
Classification: LCC LB3051 .D532 2016 | DDC 371.26--dc23 LC record available at http://
      lccn.loc.gov/2016002363

∞ ™ The paper used in this publication meets the minimum requirements of American
National Standard for Information Sciences Permanence of Paper for Printed Library
Materials, ANSI/NISO Z39.48-1992.

Printed in the United States of America

Contents

Introduction   vii

1   What Is Assessment? How Should I Use It?   1
2   Planning What to Teach   21
3   Lesson Design   37
4   Assessment Item Formats   51
5   Creating Formative Assessments   65
6   Data-Driven Decision Making: The Learning Loop   79
7   Differentiation: Content, Process, and Product   95
8   Feedback for Learning   107

References   117
Index   119
About the Author   123

Introduction

The world of teaching has dramatically changed in the last 10 years. The once autonomous life of a teacher has been replaced with a highly collaborative workplace. Teachers are expected to work together as a team to meet the differentiated needs of their students. Another change, and the most difficult one in my experience, has been the shift away from simple grading to collecting meaningful data to drive instruction. This shift has required teachers to examine student work in a new way. They are no longer simply grading work; they are looking at the strengths and the weaknesses of the student. Teachers are now required to analyze the work and determine a plan of action to help students fill the gaps in their learning. They need to be able to effectively differentiate the learning and then document the effectiveness of that differentiation. This is a much more complex analysis of student work, and many current teachers did not have this as a part of their teacher preparation. I know for myself that was the case. Most of what I was taught dealt with summative assessment to assign a grade to a student. It was largely textbook-driven. I was not taught how to create assessments that matched my students' learning outcomes. I was also not thinking about the rigor or the alignment of the content. Teachers took on faith that the textbook was aligned, and in most cases it was not. Most of the testing was at the lowest level, recall, and did not yield rich learning information. It is not a surprise because that was not the goal; the grade was the goal. It truly is an example of assessment of learning. Now, teachers are required to use assessment *for* learning (Stiggins & Chappuis, 2006). They need to be ready to use the information and not simply report it for a grade at the end of the learning segment.

This book has been created to help both the beginning and practicing teacher become more effective with the creation and analysis of classroom formative assessment. It goes one step further and will help you craft learning experiences that are standards-aligned and differentiated based on student needs, which, in my practice, is what I found was most challenging for teachers. It also includes the process of providing specific, targeted feedback to help students become more in control of their learning. It is largely informed by my own practice as a teacher and coach of teachers for the past 19 years. While I was left on my own to figure a lot of this out for myself, I want to support teachers in doing this work in a more systematic way. After reading this book, you will be able to more effectively plan units and lessons so that all students make significant progress toward the learning goals that have been established. That, after all, is what we all want in the end.

Chapter One

What Is Assessment? How Should I Use It?

As stated in the introduction, assessment is not about submitting grades at the end of the term. That might have been how it was used in the past, but grades are not the ultimate goal of assessment today. Today, the goal of assessment is to drive instructional choices so that all students are progressing. Teachers are more accountable for student learning than ever before. Principals want to see that teachers are monitoring student learning in a systematic way and making plans for acceleration or intervention when necessary. They also want to make sure that the intervention in use is successful. In fact, any school with the Response to Intervention (RtI) process must demonstrate that students are receiving the right interventions and that the interventions are working. Teachers can no longer direct their teaching to the middle level of students and hope the lower end students will get something and the high students will help the others understand. In my experience, that was the thought process of many teachers when I entered the profession. Now, teachers must see all of the students. They must demonstrate that they are effectively working with *all* students. This is why formative assessment is a critical component of success in the classroom. Teachers need to become proficient in writing and analyzing formative assessments as a means to ensure student success.

Just for a moment, let's look at the Response to Intervention process. Response to Intervention integrates both assessment and intervention. It employs a multilevel prevention system aimed at improving student achievement and reducing student behavior problems. Since behavior problems di-

1

rectly impact school success, it is important to have a system that addresses both. With the RtI framework, schools use data to identify students at risk for poor learning outcomes. It requires a systematic monitoring of student progress after the implementation of evidence-based interventions. It is expected that teachers and administrators will adjust the intensity and nature of any interventions depending on a student's responsiveness. The four essential components of this framework are screening, progress monitoring, multi-level or multitiered prevention system, and data-based decision making. I have seen this system be divided into three and four levels as demonstrated in table 1.1. Student names would be placed in the boxes in order to target interventions. A variety of assessments would be used to determine placement. State tests, district measures, and teacher-created assessments could be used together to place students.

At the bottom of the intervention worksheet is the level that all students will receive as a part of the regular day. This level is referred to as the core: school-wide programs that involve all students such as reading level grouping or a school-wide behavior modification plan. The next tier represents strategic classroom interventions that will be implemented when data shows students need support. The interventions may be agreed upon practices such as a phonics intervention for those students who demonstrate a need for a more focused or remedial approach. Everyone would be required to implement it if necessary. The third level is where you might need to add supports from outside of the classroom. This may be the resource teacher or it could be after school tutoring support. It is up to the school to develop the intervention. The top level, which should ideally have the least amount of students, is the intensive group. Students here need a more one-on-one approach. They may need special education support for academics or counseling support for behavior. I have included a link to the RtI website so that you can explore further: (http://www.rti4success.org/essential-components-rti).

While this can seem to be a daunting task, it does not have to be if the right structures are put in place. Once the foundational structure is there to do the work, it will just become the way the classroom teacher operates. The change might require a paradigm shift for some. It will certainly demand a structure of leadership that is supportive in order to make it safe for teachers to change and improve their practice. As with any change, there will be a growing period. Sometimes what teachers plan will work great and other times it will not be effective. Teachers should not be judged harshly if it does not work. They must be free to continue to try to help students succeed.

Table 1.1.   RtI Intervention Worksheet

Behavior Focus	Academic Focus
Tier 4: Intensive Students improve with the use of the universal supports and intensive classroom behavior intervention plan and supplementary support. Ideally, less students will be at this level; it represents the most intensive support required. This kind of intervention generally requires a team effort.	**Tier 4: Intensive** Students are progressing toward proficiency with universal supports and individual intensive classroom and supplementary academic interventions. The supports here might include special pull-out or push-in tutoring and special education interventions.
Tier 3: Focused Students improve with the use of the universal supports and focused intervention within the classroom with some supplementary support. Students here might need a structured plan, and the principal or other adult at the school could serve as support for success.	**Tier 3: Focused** Students are progressing toward proficiency with universal supports and focused classroom interventions and supplementary supports. Students at this level will not necessarily receive special education services, but might get tutoring services (before or after school) or small-group interventions with supplementary school personnel.
Tier 2: Strategic Students show progress using the universal supports and minor interventions. The interventions are provided within the classroom and do not require supplementary support. The students in this group might need a specific support, but will not require supplementary support. For instance, they may require specific seating, cueing, or timeout support.	**Tier 2: Strategic** Students are progressing toward proficiency with universal supports and some targeted interventions provided within the classroom. The students in this group are the ones that might be targeted for a specific intervention based upon an assessment. The teacher would monitor and adjust more frequently than with the core group.
Tier 1: Core Students have positive behavior and are fully supported by the school-wide universal supports. This level is what all students at the school will receive. This is characterized by the behavior system used throughout the school.	**Tier 1: Core** Students are progressing toward proficiency with the use of school-wide universal supports. The universal supports include differentiation, researched standards-based pedagogy, monitoring, and adjusting. Again, it is what is happening in all classrooms every day.

Using the information in this book, and planning your instruction with a learning loop in mind, will help structure the classroom so that all students are learning and there will be clear evidence of that learning. You can build the structure within your classroom even if it does not exist outside of it.

In order to assess teaching effectiveness and student learning, teachers can use both formative and summative assessments. The difference in the two types is not necessarily in content; it is in the way you intend to use the information. Let's look more closely at the two types of assessment. I will deliberately begin with formative assessment because it is ongoing and should begin before the teaching. It should also be used to monitor student understanding and create plans of action for supporting the learning. It should be, in my opinion, a daily occurrence in the classroom. It helps teachers be more effective and students more successful.

FORMATIVE ASSESSMENT

Everything teachers do in class should be based on what they learn from their students through their work. Formative assessment is the key to developing a classroom where student learning is the focus. Good formative assessment helps to determine progress toward goals for student learning and provides an opportunity for teachers to differentiate effectively for student needs. The goals are always based on the content standards. Those may be the Common Core standards or state-adopted standards. They define the learning that should be taking place in the classroom.

The goal of formative assessment is to monitor student learning toward the standards for the unit and offer an opportunity for teachers to provide targeted feedback aimed at supporting the students as they make progress toward specific and measurable goals. The goals are based upon the standards for the particular unit of study. If an assessment is given with the intention of informing the next steps of instruction, it is being used in a formative manner. The teacher will use the information to determine effectiveness of instruction, address misconceptions, and determine student readiness. The information gleaned from the assessment may also be used by the students in order to monitor their learning. This helps the students see the connection between their work and the outcome. It helps them see that they have some control over outcome. The important point to remember is that the information will change what teachers do with the students in order to meet predetermined goals laid out at the beginning of the unit.

DETERMINING EFFECTIVENESS

In order to determine the effectiveness of instruction, teachers need to develop formative assessments that are closely aligned with the standards they are teaching as a part of the unit. We, as teachers, want to know if what we taught was learned by the students. If it was not, it needs to be presented again in another manner so that students will understand. The alignment to the standard is imperative because we must be assessing exactly what we are teaching at the same level of rigor required in the standard. It is also critical that the right type of questions be asked. The questions have to be asked in a manner that allows valid inferences to be developed (Popham, 2003). The inferences made about the misconceptions will lead to the intervention. If the information collected does not allow for meaningful conclusions about the learning needs, it is not worth the time taken from instruction. Creating this type of assessment will be covered in upcoming chapters. As I stated before, this monitoring of learning is becoming more and more important. Teachers are under more and more scrutiny. Parents, administrators, and government officials are requiring evidence that teachers are instructing in an effective manner (Popham, 2003). Many school districts have adopted evaluation systems based on this idea. Creating and using standards-aligned formative assessments as a part of the instructional process will allow teachers to be proactive in demonstrating their effectiveness by documenting student progress. Using the format in this book, teachers will be able to demonstrate student learning and their plans for students who need support. I do not know a principal who would not like a teacher being able to clearly demonstrate that students are learning in their classroom, and the teacher is responding to student needs in an effective manner.

ADDRESSING MISCONCEPTIONS

Teachers can also use formative assessment to address misconceptions. Let's look at the examples below with some questions in mind. What might the misconception be? How might it be addressed?

Sample A
$2/3 + 1/5 = 3/8$
$3/5 - 1/2 = 2/3$

Sometimes students have the mistaken idea that fractions can be dealt with as separate whole numbers. They do not have the understanding of the role of the denominator (defining the number of fractional parts) and the numerator (representing the number of those parts present).

Teachers might address this issue by having meaningful experiences with fractions. They may use realia to help clarify the concept. For instance, if you use an item like an apple and pose the problem: "Keira has 3/4 of the apple and gives 1/3 to Joan. What portion of the original 3/4 does she have? If students subtracted the amounts like the sample, they will get an answer of 2/1. They will, when provided with the realia, see the impossibility of ending up with two apples when they started with less than one. This will help create an understanding of the concept of adding and subtracting fractions. This technique is especially effective with English learners and those who may have a learning difficulty. The visual component of the lesson helps them "see the math." The English learner could demonstrate the math this way even if they do not have the vocabulary necessary to fully explain.

Sample B
5 2/3 − 2 1/7 = 3

The students may not understand that the fractions need to be dealt with in a problem involving mixed numbers. They may be ignoring them because they do not know what to do with them. In order to fully understand this concept, students must understand how mixed numbers and improper fractions are related. The ability to change the mixed number to an improper fraction, and vice versa, is a critical skill. However, students need to fully understand the concept not just to be able to do countless problems. Students need to be able to express their understanding in a way that demonstrates they understand the meaning of the expression. Providing visuals would help struggling students understand the concept in a more concrete manner.

The one thing I would change about the above assessments is to give students a chance to express their thinking in words or pictures. First of all, this is a consideration for students who struggle communicating in English. They have the option of drawing a picture to demonstrate understanding. If students are asked to explain their thinking, it gives the teacher an opportunity to hone in on the particular misconception. The simple addition of asking students to explain opens up an avenue for more information about their learning. This change will lead to more valid inferences and a more specific intervention plan.

Now, the above problems came from an elementary level math program, but the same thinking process can be used to determine the misconceptions at any level. The point is to think about what the students are controlling and what they do not fully understand in the process. That helps define the misconceptions and then you are able to design an intervention to address the specific misconception. The misconceptions vary with the mathematical content, but the analytical process remains the same.

Try It: As an exercise, take the above problems and create a small group lesson that helps the students deal with the misconceptions. How might you get them to understand the meaning of the numerator and the denominator? What would you focus on first? How might you monitor the understanding? If the above standards do not apply to your work, use student work to determine the misconception and then create a plan.

DETERMINING READINESS

When I was in school, teachers taught and then tested. Students were given several tests throughout the semester and the grades were averaged. This might have occurred weekly or every other week. Generally it occurred at the end of a chapter or unit. Students either succeeded or failed. If they failed, they were not provided feedback and another opportunity to learn. The teacher was moving on. It often affirmed the mind-set that students were either gifted with math ability or not. That is not a valid inference. Too many students were left behind in this model. I would have to say I was one of them. My worst subject in school was math. The instruction made no sense to me, and the teacher was not formatively assessing as we went. When the test came, I failed. I was only presented the information one way and was never given specific feedback on the parts of the problem solving I was having trouble understanding. It was not until college that I had an instructor who used formative assessment and gave me feedback so that I was able to comprehend. I went from feeling like a failure to an A student in my math classes. Don't we want all of our students to feel successful as learners? Then we have to help them succeed by effectively diagnosing the problems they are having and creating a support for the students to move along in the learning process. This is true in any content area and at any grade level.

Every student is not ready for the same instruction at the same time. A teacher needs to determine where the students are, in the learning of the content, and then plan accordingly. It is not a safe assumption to think that all students are ready for grade-level content just because they are in the class. There are too many variables in play. Students come from different school backgrounds, they may have a language barrier, or they may have a learning style that must be taken into account to increase the learning potential. Not all 10-year-olds are at the exact same development level. Why would we assume that one type of learning experience, generally teacher driven, would work for all students? Based on my own experience, I would say it works for few students.

One of the simplest structures for using assessment in a formative manner for readiness is the pre-assessment, instruction, and post-assessment model. The pretest is a diagnostic assessment. It allows a teacher to determine readiness (screening from RtI) and see the strengths and weaknesses of the students before beginning instruction. Teachers need to know where the students are at the beginning. The assessment piece should be teacher created and aligned to the standards in use. In my practice, the textbook adoptions came with pretests and posttests. However, they were often selected response and did not yield rich understanding of the misconceptions. Students just circled the answer and did not always attempt the problem. You will learn, in later chapters, how to write meaningful assessments that align with the standards you are using. This will provide a glimpse into the thinking of the student, and that is what you need to determine misconceptions.

To begin the process, the teacher gives a test over the content he or she is planning to teach (fractions). The test covers all of the material that will be taught. Students take the test, and are told to do the best that they can. "This will help me plan our learning." This assessment *is not graded*; it is analyzed by the teacher to plan the instruction. The results will tell the teacher where to begin and how to group students for learning. It may also indicate that some of the material is already mastered by all students. That saves time. If they already know it, don't teach it. Instead, use that time for what they don't know. Time is a precious commodity in a classroom. If teachers had used this format in my day, they would have been able to use the information on the pretest to group me for learning. They could have more effectively addressed my misunderstandings. They would have been able to recognize the students who needed support, the students who were ready to learn the content, and the students who needed acceleration because they already had the skill. Those who needed acceleration in my math classes did not get it, and they were most likely bored. They had to do what they already knew.

Determining student readiness for instruction is critical for success. If teachers are expecting students to learn, they must make sure the students have the precursor knowledge to build upon. If they do not, that is where to start. The learning must be effectively scaffolded so that the students are supported in the learning. You would never expect a house to be built without a firm foundation. Students must have a foundation of knowledge on which to build their learning. If they have pieces missing, that must be addressed before they can be expected to understand the content fully. Teachers must also determine if students already know what they are planning to teach. If they know it, teachers have an obligation to help those students accelerate or deepen their learning. Some of our students take the pretest and can clearly demonstrate an understanding of the content. Students who are proficient in a topic deserve instruction that will engage them in a meaningful way. Teachers need to be able to support them to go further or deeper into the learning. Oftentimes, students like this get chosen as the peer tutors. That is a perfectly good strategy at times, but it is not helping the proficient students move deeper in their learning. This is when a teacher might look at the standards for the next grade to plan some acceleration for students.

The pre/post structure is good for a short unit—something that you might be teaching over one week, perhaps. However, if you are teaching a unit that is several weeks long or that is multidisciplinary, this model will not suffice in my opinion. In order to provide meaningful feedback to students about their learning, teachers have to include several opportunities for students to demonstrate their learning. There would need to be several formative assessments prior to the posttest in order to direct the teaching and support students' learning. The formative assessments in the middle of the unit will enable students to receive corrective feedback aimed at supporting the attainment of the standard.

TYPES OF FORMATIVE ASSESSMENTS

There are a variety of assignments that could be considered formative assessments. Anecdotal notes, discussions (Think-Pair-Share, small group), white boards, exit slips, questioning, and Jot Thoughts are a few structures that would allow teachers to monitor understanding (Kagan & Kagan, 2009). There are several excellent sites that give more examples. A simple search on the Internet will result in a plethora of ideas.

Anecdotal notes are taken by the teacher as the students engage in group or individual work. They may also be notes jotted down as a result of looking at student work. Generally, it is best to be focused upon one aspect of the learning while taking the notes. This will allow the teacher to develop targeted and specific feedback for the student. There are several ways to organize the notes. There is no right or wrong way—whatever works best for the individual teacher. I have seen both sticky notes and 4 x 5 cards work well. The point is that the information is used to make changes to the instruction based upon the student needs. If your notes are showing you that some students are having trouble with a certain step in the solving of a math problem, you address that step: not the whole process, but that piece of the process where they are stuck. You are trying to move them to the next level, not just having them practice. The error will be more difficult to correct if they continue to practice incorrectly. The anecdotal notes can also be used to articulate student learning to a principal or parent.

Discussions are a bit tricky but can be used effectively to determine what students know and where they are struggling. Whole-group discussions rarely allow enough interaction of every individual to get a true sense of understanding. The quiet ones get lost because the more assertive students tend to dominate. Small-group discussions can work, but they must be structured. The careful use of structures like Think-Pair-Share or Numbered Heads, which are both Kagan and Kagan (2009) cooperative learning structures, can be helpful. Each student is required to participate and the teacher can listen with a specific focus in mind. The teacher can intervene right away and use questions to help correct or solidify learning. That would be instant feedback. Caution should be used here in that students should not feel that they are being corrected in front of others. Instead, the teacher should become part of the conversation in a meaningful way to help all understand. It is something teachers become better at with practice.

White boards can be used to determine student understanding. One caution is to make sure that students are actually working on their own so they are demonstrating their understanding. One way to do that is by having the students numbered. You might have students in groups of four. Initially you might give a problem to practice and each number would get a different problem.

1: $345 + 236$
2: $546 + 127$
3: $127 + 347$

4: 765 + 126

The teacher could then use observation to see which students are struggling and which might be ready to move on to a more difficult problem. I have also seen this work well in upper grades where students are up and working on the large white boards in the classroom. This provides the necessary space to solve more complex problems. The point is that all are engaged in finding solutions to a variety of problems in a way that the teacher can observe the process he or she is utilizing and coach if necessary.

Exit tickets work in much the same manner. Each individual is required to do an example. In language class, for example, if the lesson is compound sentences, the teacher might require that the student write a compound sentence using a conjunction. There will be a variety of responses, but it is a quick look to tell who can do it and who cannot. Students could be asked to write a short paragraph to explain their thinking about a story's theme or the author's purpose. In math class, they might be creating and solving one problem. This assessment should be quick. It should not take more than 5 minutes. It is a way to wrap up something that has been taught and determine if students understand the concept. Again, it is not something that will be graded but rather something that will inform the next steps to take with individuals or the whole group in the next learning session. By holistically analyzing the work, it will enable feedback to be provided or plans to be made to address any misconceptions. It might be as simple as creating a "got it" and a "didn't get it" pile. The "didn't get it" pile would be the one to analyze for misconceptions. Those are the students you might call back to work in a small group or work with individually in the next learning segment. This group should be relatively small if the instruction was effective. If it is most of the class, the instruction was not effective and the learning should occur again with a new approach.

Questioning can be occurring as a part of interactive collaborative learning or discussions. Teachers can be joining in on the conversation and interjecting questions that help determine student understanding or help students delve deeper into the thinking about the topic. Some of those questions should be preplanned by the instructor so they are ready. A variety of questions should be used. Teachers should use both open and closed questions. An open question is one with a variety of possible answers. There is not one single right response. A closed question requires a short answer and no elaboration. It might be simply a recalling of information.

Open Questions

- How do you think those who disagree with you might respond to your argument?
- What might happen if (fill in the blank) were outlawed? (guns, fast food)

Closed Questions

- Who was the 16th president of the United States?
- What is the numerator of the fraction?

When using questioning there are a few considerations. One is to not make your questions leading in any way. They should stimulate the thinking and discussion of the students without interjecting bias. The teacher must take a neutral position. It is about getting the students to think, not getting them to think like the teacher. A teacher should be ready to approach any issue from both sides effectively. Another consideration is to listen to the whole response. Oftentimes the teacher sees where the student is going and wants to interject. Resist that impulse! Students might see their own reasoning errors if they are allowed to process them completely. Many students need to verbally process their thinking and are rarely allowed the opportunity to do so. They will learn more by going through the thinking rather than being told by the instructor. Some people benefit from verbal processing, and we often do not allow that to happen. We just want to get to the answer and then move on. Lastly, remember to give the student a little silent time to respond. Students need a little time to process and formulate their responses. Waiting 5–10 seconds will increase the likelihood of a better response. It will also demonstrate that the students must do the thinking—the teacher will not supply the answer. If students are struggling to answer, try rephrasing the question rather than supplying an answer. The goal is to guide the students to be able to express their thinking.

Try It: Think of three open and closed questions you could use in a classroom. Share them with your colleagues. Why are they good? Can they be better?

While discussions and questioning are useful to get a glimpse of student understanding, it is important to give the student an opportunity for individual response. One way of doing that is by employing a Jot Thoughts, which is another Kagan and Kagan (2009) structure. While Kagan used it for brainstorming, I have modified it to use in the classroom for a little more substantive response. It should not take more than 10 minutes. I usually reserved it for the end of a lesson. In order to check for understanding, the questions should be crafted around your focus of the lesson.

- What do you think will happen next in the story and why?
- 2/3 + 1/5: Solve and explain how you solved the problem using words or pictures.
- What is one character trait you would use to describe Wilbur in *Charlotte's Web*? Why?

The questions will allow the teacher to determine if students are catching on to the lesson. Can they identify a character trait and support it with evidence? Can the students convert and solve a fraction problem with unlike denominators? Can they make a logical prediction about a fiction text? The previous questions are based on language taken directly from grade-level standards. If students are not able to do the task, the teacher will have information that will allow him to tailor instruction for individual student learning. The results may allow the teacher to group students for instruction based on common misconceptions. It is not about grading the assessment to assign a grade; it is about discovering student understanding. Formative assessments should help teachers know more about their students and help students succeed in their learning.

SUMMATIVE ASSESSMENT

The ultimate goal of a summative assessment is to measure the level of proficiency that has been obtained by the student at the end of an instructional unit. It compares the student work against some standard or benchmark. Some examples of this type of assessment include a final exam that assigns a grade to a report card, an evaluation of a final project or speech on a topic, a district benchmark, end-of-chapter tests, and state-mandated tests. Summative assessments are often high stakes and have a high point value attached to them. In the case of state-mandated tests, they can have far-reaching implications. Schools can be sanctioned as a result of poor performance on such tests. I have worked at three such schools. Due to persistent failure, the schools were restructured in order to change the results. The results were changed at all of them by instituting a solid formative assessment program.

The schools also devoted time to allow teachers to work together to analyze student work and create intervention plans that addressed the needs of the students.

A final exam is often cumulative in nature and requires students to demonstrate a complete understanding of the topic. Remember that the formative assessments measure specific parts of the topic. They are more targeted on providing feedback, not grading. The results of summative assessments are used to assign a grade for the semester or year. They are often, but not exclusively, created as selected response. Other question types such as short answers, matching, and binary choice can be used as well. There are some times when the learning needs to be evaluated for a final grade, which is the role of the summative assessment. The calendar tells us when the end of the semester comes and grades must be turned in at that point. If it is not the last semester of the year, students have an opportunity to improve still, but if it is the end of the year, there is no time for change. That final grade may be used by the next teacher as a starting point for the next school year, but the current teacher will not be making intervention plans based upon the results; that criterion makes them summative. Remember it is about how the information is used.

The state-mandated tests given at the end of the school year are summative rather than formative because they are given too late for there to be any real change in instruction based upon them. When teachers get the scores for their classes, they cannot use them to plan for the upcoming classes because they are getting new students. While they might be able to make some basic decisions about the new students they are getting by looking at the scores from their previous year, they were based on different grade-level standards and they may not be accurate for the expectations of the new grade level. If they are used to make some basic decisions about the beginning of the year, teachers will have to monitor and adjust when the work of the school year starts.

Some people say that a summative test, generally this means the state tests, can be used to determine effectiveness of instruction. I am cautious about that use for some summative assessments. First of all, the assessments were probably written by someone far removed from the classroom (Shepard, 2001). They may test what has been covered in the class and they may not. The writers may have unpacked the standards before constructing the test, but they may not have written the items at the correct level of rigor. There may be a difference in the understanding of the standards. The teacher who is presenting the information may have understood the level of proficiency in a standard much differently than the person who created the test. Testing rule number one is this: test what you are actually teaching. When you do not control the test, you cannot guarantee that it is totally aligned to what was taught.

Another problem with standardized tests is that they are largely selected response and do not allow students to demonstrate their full understanding. They have to choose the best answer, and that often trips them up. That might not be giving a true picture of the student's understanding if that is the only tool. It is worthwhile to note that the current tests being developed for the Common Core are incorporating some of the explaining I described previously. The questions do allow students to express their understanding beyond a selected response format. However, there is not enough evidence yet that those tests will be any more valid. It remains to be seen. Therefore, it is impossible to tell if it is the test format or the lack of understanding that is causing a student to do poorly on the test. There are other issues like language acquisition that enter into the equation as well. For example, students may not have the academic language proficiency to perform on this kind of test. Teachers may have helped students make substantial progress, but it will not show up on this particular test. Many scholars such as James Popham (1999) agree that teacher effectiveness should not be measured by state-mandated tests in their current form. Good formative assessment is a better measure of instructional effectiveness and a more useful tool for program effectiveness.

Summative and formative assessment should be used together to determine student learning over time. The better aligned each assessment is to the targeted learning goals, the more informative they will be for current and future practice. While districts and teachers have limited voice in the construction of state tests, district tests can, and should, be tightly aligned to the understood learning goals and agreed upon standards. That has the potential to aid in the evaluation of the effectiveness of intervention programs and teacher effectiveness. However, teachers need to be involved in the process of creating the summative assessments. They cannot be developed by people who are far from the classroom and are not engaged deeply in the work of learning. This teacher input is happening in some schools and districts. Teacher teams are being called upon to develop standards-based summative assessments. This, in my opinion, should be happening everywhere. Top-down implementation does not generally go well and does not lead to all being invested in the work. If you want a group to care about the results, give them a say in the creation of the measurement tool.

High-stakes summative assessments are largely out of the control of the classroom teacher. They are a reality, but cannot be used to drive the instruction. If there is a structure used in the classroom to assess and provide effective feedback for learning, the state tests will take care of themselves. You will see a marked improvement because the students have been taught to think and work through difficulty. I speak from experience. In my second turnaround, my grade level was the most successful. As you can see in table 1.2, the class entering 4th grade in 2007 only had 13% of the students proficient in English. That group left my team at 64% proficient. The following group went from 30% to 74% proficient (Dial, 2011). That result is directly related to this process. It works!

VALIDITY

No matter what assessment you are employing, the validity of the instrument must be taken into consideration. Validity is the ability of the instrument to actually measure what it is supposed to measure. There are three kinds of validity evidence considered when evaluating assessments: criterion, construct, and content. "Each type, usually collected via some sort of investigation or analytic effort, contributes to the conclusion that a test is yielding data that will support valid inferences" (Popham, 2003). Two of the validity measures are really out of the scope of a classroom teacher's job. Construct and criterion validity are best left to the assessment specialists. Classroom teachers do not have the time or the expertise to determine if an assessment has construct or criterion validity. However, teachers should be somewhat familiar with these forms of validity because they will be asked to make inferences based on assessments created out of the class by testing companies and district personnel. It would be appropriate to think about the validity of those tests. Since inferences about student learning and teacher performance

Table 1.2.   Team Success

Year	2nd Grade	3rd Grade	4th Grade	5th Grade	6th Grade
2007	20%	13%	61%	19%	36%
2008	40%	30%	64%	52%	40%
2009	40%	31%	74%	70%	78%

might be made based on high-stakes testing, it is important to think about the validity of the instruments used to make those inferences.

Criterion Validity

This kind of validity is generally beyond the daily tasks of teachers. It requires giving the test to many similar groups and then determining if the test is a valid predictor of the construct that you are measuring. One example is whether aptitude tests, like the SAT or ACT, truly predict what they claim to predict. If the relationship between the tests scores and the college grade point averages of the students is strong, then the results support making the inference about success of students with high scores on the test having success in college (Popham, 2003). The high scores were predictive of the individual's subsequent success in college.

Construct Validity

Construct validity is the experimental demonstration that a test is measuring the construct it claims to be measuring. Generally, the experiment takes the form of a differential-groups study. This requires that the performances on

Table 1.3.   Types of Validity

Type of Validity	Definition	Example
Content	The extent to which the content of the assessment matches the instructional objectives.	A semester or quarter exam that only includes content covered during the last six weeks is not a valid measure of the course's overall objectives—it has very low content validity.
Criterion	The extent to which the scores on the test agree with (concurrent validity) or predict (predictive validity) an external criterion.	If the end-of-year math tests in 4th grade correlate highly with the statewide math tests, they would have high concurrent validity.
Construct	The extent to which an assessment corresponds to other variables, as predicted by some rationale or theory.	If you can correctly hypothesize that ESOL students will perform differently on a reading test than English-speaking students, the assessment may have construct validity.

the test are compared for two groups: one that has the construct and one that does not have the construct. If the group with the construct performs better than the group without the construct, that result is said to provide evidence of the construct validity of the test. If a test measuring algebra skills was administered to math majors, who presumably took math all through high school, and also given to college students who had not taken math since their freshman year in high school, the prediction would be that the majors would do better on the test. If the results confirmed that, then the instrument would have construct validity. The instrument would be measuring college students' math skills (Popham, 2003). This kind of validity is similar to criterion in that teachers do not have the time to do the investigations necessary to determine construct validity. There are many approaches to collecting evidence of construct validity, but it is best left to assessment specialists.

Content Validity

For the purposes of formative classroom assessment, this is a critical piece, and in control of the individual teacher or teacher team. The test should test the content that has been covered in the class. It should also be written at the level of difficulty required by the standards covered in the unit. This requires unpacking of the standards, which will be covered in depth in other chapters. It must also be in a format that allows valid inferences to be made about the student's ability in the content. For instance, if I want to determine if a student can solve a multistep math problem, I have to have a format that allows the student to show her work. A multiple choice item will not necessarily do that. The student may simply guess, which does not give accurate information about her understanding. This test creation will be covered more in depth in later chapters.

As you can see in table 1.3, content validity is impacted by what items are included on the assessment. If you are intending to write a summative assessment for a learning unit or semester, all learning for the time period must be included in the assessment. If the assessment items only come from a portion of the semester, there is low content validity. It will not accurately demonstrate the entire learning period. If you are writing a formative assessment for part of the learning unit, you would not include items you had not taught. This will become clearer as you create assessments in later chapters.

CONCLUSION

Both formative and summative assessment should have a place in the classroom. They should be used together to create a fuller picture of student learning and teacher effectiveness. They must be carefully created and enable teachers to provide students feedback that helps drive the learning forward. In order to make sound instructional decisions, the assessments used must be valid. We have to be testing what we intend to test. Teachers, administrators, parents, and students need to be critical consumers of assessment information. Everyone has a part in creating schools that enable students to succeed.

DISCUSSION QUESTIONS

1. What is the value of good formative assessments?
2. What structures might need to be in place for teachers to create and analyze formative assessments?
3. What are some solutions to the obstacles that might be present in the current structure?

Chapter Two

Planning What to Teach

"If you fail to plan, you are planning to fail!"—Benjamin Franklin

I begin with the quote by Benjamin Franklin to stress the importance of effective planning in teaching. When you watch good teachers, it is not always easy to see their planning. Believe me, it is there. They have spent time thinking about what they plan to teach and how they will teach it. They have considered both the scope (what must be covered) and the sequence (in what order it will be covered). They also have thought about the possible outcomes of the learning they have planned. What might the students need? What are the possible misunderstandings? Thinking like this enables them to react in a way that extends the learning for those who are likely to know the material and supports the learning for those who might have some difficulty. They might take the students deeper into the content, or they might have to go back a step to help them build a more complete understanding. In any case, they are ready to react because of their planning. They are being proactive rather than reactive. This simple change will alleviate a lot of stress for the teacher and the student.

FOCUSING THE CONTENT

For the purposes of planning, it is important to first decide what it is that you will be teaching over the course of the year. The number of standards required at each grade level is hardly achievable. There are too many to use as assessment targets. In order to focus the work in the classroom, I recommend evaluating the standards for a grade level using the criteria shared by James Popham (2003) in his book *Test Better, Teach Better: The Instructional Role of Assessment*. He advocates assigning each of the standards a rating: essential, highly desirable, or desirable. Larry Ainsworth (2003a and 2003b) has also done extensive work in this area. He refers to them as power standards. He would add the ideas of endurance, leverage, and readiness to the evaluation criteria. I think both descriptions are necessary to really examine standards. Let's look at each of these and the criteria used to determine the rating of a standard.

Essential

If a standard is essential, it is something that is absolutely necessary for the student to master by the end of the instruction. This is supported by the work of Larry Ainsworth (2003a and 2003b). These are the standards that build from year to year. Without mastery of the essential standards, students will have a difficult time succeeding in subsequent learning. These standards will focus more on teachable skills such as writing a powerfully persuasive piece in writing. It is not merely knowledge based like knowing the difference between a noun and a verb. While that is important to craft a well-written sentence, it is the writing of the piece that is the most critical. In this case, the sentence creation and the crafting of a position are the necessary criteria. Ainsworth suggests that the essential standards have endurance. They are something that is needed beyond the test. Learning this content will be important to the student's future success. If there is lifelong value, the standard has endurance. For demonstration purposes, I am using a Common Core standard here, but a state-developed standard could be substituted. Here are some examples:

CCSS.ELA-Literacy.W.4.4
   Produce clear and coherent writing in which the development and organization are appropriate to task, purpose, and audience.

CCSS.ELA-Literacy.W.8.4
   Produce clear and coherent writing in which the development, organization, and style are appropriate to task, purpose, and audience (grade-specific expectations for arguments, expository, and narrative texts)

The above standards would be considered essential. Whatever the genre of the writing, students must be able to produce clear and coherent writing that aligns with the purpose. It also qualifies for endurance because every person should be able to clearly and coherently communicate for a specific purpose. It is a standard that continues with the students throughout schooling. It clearly continues on through middle and high school using the same language. This is a skill that has lifelong implications. If students are not able to do this effectively, they are limited in their options. For instance, they will not likely get into college without the ability to write an organized essay, which is part of many college applications. They also are not likely to rise into management in any kind of job if they are not able to communicate both verbally and in writing in a coherent manner. It is therefore essential for all students to master this standard.

Ainsworth (2003a and 2003b) also considers the leverage of the standard. Will it prove to be valuable in learning other content or in other academic areas? If it will, it has leverage and should be considered essential. Let's consider the above standard again. How might it relate or support other learning? I would say that it extends into math, social studies, science, and reading. For example, in order to clearly demonstrate understanding, students will need to be able to use this skill to craft an answer to a question or explain the historical significance of an event. If they are asked to explain a scientific process, they will have to be able to do so in a clear and coherent manner. Organization of the writing will matter in both examples in order to achieve clarity of the message.

Lastly, Ainsworth asks us to look at readiness. Is this knowledge or skill something that the student needs to be successful and achieve not only in this grade level but in subsequent grades? If the answer is yes to that question, and I argue that it is in the example standard, it meets the readiness criteria. We will expect the complexity of the writing to grow as students proceed from grade to grade, but being clear and coherent in their written communication is something students will need throughout their schooling and work life.

Highly Desirable

The second rating for a standard, according to Popham (2003), is whether it is highly desirable. A highly desirable standard is very important for the student to master by the end of the instruction period. These, along with the essential standards, must be included in your planning. The highly desirable standards often support the essential standards. Let's go back to our example:

CCSS.ELA-Literacy.W.4.4

Produce clear and coherent writing in which the development and organization are appropriate to task, purpose, and audience.

If the above standard is essential for students to master, then the components that will make the writing clear and coherent must be included and focused upon. By focusing on the building blocks, teachers can give specific and meaningful feedback to the students on those components. That feedback, which will be discussed in later chapters, will help the student move toward proficiency in the essential standards. In the following second example, standards should be included in the planning to support the essential writing standard:

CCSS.ELA-Literacy.W.4.1.a

Introduce a topic or text clearly, state an opinion, and create an organizational structure in which related ideas are grouped to support the writer's purpose.

CCSS.ELA-Literacy.W.4.1.b

Provide reasons that are supported by facts and details.

CCSS.ELA-Literacy.W.4.1.d

Provide a concluding statement or section related to the opinion presented.

In order to create that clear, coherent writing, students will need an effective topic sentence that helps to establish the purpose of the writing, be able to support their assertions with facts and details, and be able to conclude the writing that relates to the information presented. As I always told my students, you can't just leave readers hanging; you need to wrap it up for them. All of these skills can be easily monitored through formative assessment. Concentrate on these skills when providing meaningful feedback; the writing, then, will become clear and coherent, thus achieving the essential standard.

Desirable

The final rating Popham (2003) suggests is whether a standard is desirable. To be considered desirable, the standard would be something the teacher would like students to master, but it would not be critical. It is something that we hope to develop, but a student can find success in life without it. I ask you to consider the following example:

CCSS.ELA-Literacy.W.4.10

Write routinely over extended time frames (time for research, reflection, and revision) and shorter time frames (a single sitting or a day or two) for a range of discipline-specific tasks, purposes, and audiences.

While I write for a variety of purposes on a daily basis, not everyone does. I didn't even always do it. When I was a business owner, I rarely communicated in writing. Most of my interactions were oral. I certainly did not devote time every day to writing. Many adults do not. Some jobs require this, and some do not. I think it is something all teachers hope to create in their students. Ultimately, we want our students to be lifelong readers and writers. You hear it all the time, but the reality is not everyone is a lifelong reader or writer. It is possible to have a good life and never master this standard. That is what makes it desirable in my opinion. It is also something I will not assess. It might be the way I frame my writing block, but I will not be assessing this skill.

Try It: Use your state standards or the Common Core standards and take a look at one grade level. Determine your ratings for the standards listed. Why have you rated them the way you have? What makes them priority standards for you? What about them is enduring or essential? Why are the ones you determine as desirable in that category? This work will be built upon in the next chapters so keep track of those standards you have determined to be essential and highly desirable. They are the ones that you will plan with in chapter 3 and build assessments for in chapters 4 and 5.

LONG- AND SHORT-TERM PLANNING

New teachers are likely to be in the "survival mode" during their first year. There is so much to do, and it is likely that they feel overwhelmed by it all. They are often making only short-term decisions. Long-term planning is focused on decisions that relate to academic goals. Where should the students be in a month or in two months? Using the curriculum and the textbook are excellent starting points for helping plan the learning goals for the grade level team.

Planning can focus on the short term or long term. Short-term planning concentrates on what will be accomplished in a day or a week. It is a well-thought-out plan for the week that includes formative assessment to measure the impact of the instruction and the level of student understanding. It is not just putting down the page numbers of the book you intend to read or the pages you will cover in math. The inclusion of formative assessment is to help pace and differentiate the learning so all students are making adequate progress toward the ultimate goal. The short-term planning allows for reflection on daily class interactions and making changes based on that reflection. The reflection and the decisions should be made with the long-term plan in mind. If that plan is not considered, there is a potential for getting off track and moving away from the ultimate goal. I have provided an example of this at the end of the chapter. It will help to demonstrate how to think about the week's lessons in a way that focuses on the learning and the assessment of that learning.

It is important to remember that reflection is not a formal process a teacher must go through every day. Good teachers think about what went well and what didn't. Having some work that helps demonstrate that you are correct about your assumptions just adds support for your decisions. If an administrator asks a question about your teaching, the student work will provide evidence for the discussion. What I am advocating for here is a quick assessing of the students through meaningful activities. Remember the work does not need to be graded in detail; it needs to be holistically evaluated. This kind of evaluation can be accomplished by thinking about some general questions.

- What did my students master today? How do I know?
- What seems to be the misunderstandings? How are the misunderstandings best addressed?
- Are there any that need to move on/be remediated? What is the best way to address their needs?

Thinking about the work with the guiding questions will help with the creation of differentiation plans for the groups of students in the class. The decisions are based on what the students demonstrated. Not all students will need remediation, but some will. That needs to be addressed in order for the students to make the necessary progress. Without a solid plan of dealing with the misunderstandings, the students will not be able to build the bridges they need to fully comprehend the content. It is important to remember that short-term planning is fluid and flexible. The plan will change based on the information from the formative assessments. The better the assessments, the better the information you have to base learning decisions upon. The creation of good questions and assessments will be covered in detail later.

Long-term planning takes the plan to a whole month or possibly the entire year. You have to know where you are going if you are going to get there. You need to know the content standards that you must master this year. That is why we have determined which are essential and highly desirable. You would not take a road trip without having a destination. As a part of the trip, you plan stopping points along the way. Those stopping points might change as you progress on your trip. You might hit road construction and have to take a detour, but you make decisions based on the final destination. What will it take to get there? How do I get around this obstacle? Teaching is no different. You need a road map of how you will accomplish the learning for the year. You need to have an idea of how you will proceed, but you have to be willing to change if you have students who are not understanding along the way. You have to help them get around the detour and reach that final destination. Your short-term plans will help with that adjustment. The long-term plan is not written in stone; it can be changed based on information gained from formative assessments and observations. For example, the grade-level team may have allotted two weeks for some learning and, through assessment, find that the students do not need that amount of time. They can adjust and use the time to add to future learning. There is no point to stay on the topic once it is mastered: move on.

This is one reason I always had great difficulty with district pacing guides and curriculum pacing guides in any reading or math adoption. They were generally written by someone out of the classroom. It represented the time they thought the students would need, but they did not know, or work with, my students. The guide writers had no idea what knowledge the students arrived with or how quickly they mastered a concept. While I always met the goal of the semester, I generally did it in a different pace than was suggested by the district because it was demanded by the learners in my classroom. They were the focus of all of my decisions, and those decisions were based upon data. Why stress them and me out trying to fit some arbitrary schedule? I could easily defend my decisions if asked by an administrator because I could produce data from formative assessment that would clearly support my instructional choices.

Long-term planning is generally done by a grade-level team. Most schools have some sort of collaboration process that grade levels use, and this planning is part of that process. It is important that all teachers know where they are going and the plan for getting there. If the team will be using formative assessments, they have to give them at the same time in order to analyze them and provide intervention. They might want to group the students for intervention across the grade level. If one teacher did not finish the assessment, he or she will not know what the needs of their students are and will not be able to participate in the intervention. The formative assessment also helps to determine effectiveness. One teacher on a team might get fantastic results with a concept. It will be important in team meetings to talk about that and share effective pedagogy. Those conversations make all of the teachers better. In order to do that, they must all be getting through the curriculum in the same time frame. I am not advocating for cookie-cutter classrooms. Each classroom will be unique, because each teacher brings his or her own strengths to the work. I am advocating for the program to be solid and agreed upon. There will not be huge differences between the classroom demographics at one school. The students will proceed at approximately the same rate. Being together will allow teachers to provide remediation or acceleration as a team. They can be creative in grouping students for time periods during the day that allow for that differentiation of learning. It should be a collaborative decision based on the needs of the students.

A long-term plan should be laid out in clear format. I have seen calendars work well for this planning. It should list out the units that will be taught and the standards that will be the focus for the work. In order to determine the focus standards, teachers will have to determine the essential standards. You will also have timetables for the formative assessments. In most schools, teams are asked to collaborate on a regular basis. In order to make that time effective, teachers need to bring student work for conversation. This kind of document will help the team stay on track and complete the formative assessments so that they may be discussed and gaps identified. This is a tentative schedule, and it can be changed based upon the results from the formative assessments. The standards to be assessed for the unit will be those standards previously identified by the team.

Long-term planning also incorporates pedagogy decisions. What strategies will best serve the purpose? Is cooperative learning a strategy that will aid in the development of understanding? Students will have to be able to work more cooperatively if that is the case. The students will need several opportunities in pairs and small groups. It is gradual and must be structured and planned. The students will need specific feedback on the skills required as well. They will need reinforcement about active listening, compromise, and communication. In order to effectively do that, it must be planned as a part of the instruction.

The calendar in figure 2.1 shows an outline for reading, writing, and math. It demonstrates how you would put in opportunities for grade-level assessments that will help you see what the students are mastering. I will discuss fully how to craft those assessments in chapters 4 and 5. The standards I have listed are the ones I will assess. Notice the assessments are "chunked." There is a clear focus so that I am able to provide feedback on the learning. For instance, in the first week of writing instruction, there would be a focus on the topic sentence, the details, and using specific vocabulary. That is what the students will receive feedback about. In the second week, the focus will be on the concluding statement and the linking of ideas. I might provide further feedback on the other elements, but the focus will be on the elements that were the instructional focus for the week. I will not be grading the entire essay in detail every week. It is not possible. I am providing coaching on the building blocks of the essay by concentrating my focus on the elements for the week. The reading comprehension skills are imbedded in the writing. It is how I will assess whether the students understand the story. The writing will provide the evidence of comprehension because the questions will be crafted in such a way that it leads the students to demonstrate understanding. Remember, time is short. Make every assignment count in a variety of ways.

It is important to plan the week's lesson around what students can actually do, keeping the long-term target in mind. The daily and weekly plans shown in the calendar address the components of the learning. For instance, in the writing example in figure 2.1, the following are the standards that will be focused upon for this month:

CCSS.ELA-Literacy.W.4.2
Write informative/explanatory texts to examine a topic and convey ideas and information clearly.

☐ December	~ January 2014 ~					February ☐
Sun	**Mon**	**Tue**	**Wed**	**Thu**	**Fri**	**Sat**
			1	2	3	4
5	6 School Resumes Math: Fractions Equivalence, ordering Pretest given– Focus Standards: CCSS4NFA1, A2,C5,C6 ELA: Begin Comprehension- Non-Fiction Text RI 4.1, 4.2, 4.4 RI 4.7 Writing: Explanatory Writing ELA–Literacy 4.2 A,B,C,D,E	7	8	9	10 Formative Assessment Math A1, A2	11
12	13	14	15 Formative Writing Assessment– Using science reading about spiders and insects– 4.2 A.B, D RI 4.1, 4.2, 4.4, 4.7 assessed in the writing.	16	17 Formative Assessment C5,C6	18
19	20 MLK Day	21	22 Formative Writing Assessment– Using science reading about mammals and reptiles 4.2 C, E RI 4.1, 4.2, 4.4, 4.7 assessed in the writing.	23	24 Summative Assessment A1, A2, C5, C6	25
26	27 Fractions: Adding, Subtracting, Multiplying, Dividing–Focus Standards B3A, B3C,B3D, B4, B4A, B4B ,B4C– Pretest	28	29	30	31 Reading Comprehension Summative Assessment– Cold read/Writing	Notes:

Figure 2.1.   Calendar.

CCSS.ELA-Literacy.W.4.2.a

Introduce a topic clearly and group related information in paragraphs and sections; include formatting (e.g., headings), illustrations, and multimedia when useful to aiding comprehension.

CCSS.ELA-Literacy.W.4.2.b

Develop the topic with facts, definitions, concrete details, quotations, or other information and examples related to the topic.

CCSS.ELA-Literacy.W.4.2.c

Link ideas within categories of information using words and phrases (e.g., *another, for example, also, because*).

CCSS.ELA-Literacy.W.4.2.d

Use precise language and domain-specific vocabulary to inform about or explain the topic.

CCSS.ELA-Literacy.W.4.2.e

Provide a concluding statement or section related to the information or explanation presented.

Although the overall goal of the unit is the writing of informative and explanatory texts, it is important to have a plan to address the components. For the first week, the lessons should focus on a, b, and d. That is what will be formatively assessed the next week. The teachers will have seven days to plan and teach before that formative assessment opportunity.

In the weekly plan, the students will need a model of the skills that will be taught and expected to be mastered. I am structuring this explanation as a Think Aloud. I am trying to let you, the reader, glimpse inside my thought process here. I want to make what and why I am doing things clear. The reading and writing standards are used to guide this plan.

Day 1

Reading: Model finding the main idea and determining the meaning of unknown words (4.2, 4.4). I am starting here because students must be able to determine the main idea in order to formulate a topic sentence. This skill will help them formulate a more effective topic sentence. That will be my writing focus on the same day.

Provide time for students to work in partners or triads with the goal of determining the main idea and the meaning of unknown words based on context. Each group will receive a different reading passage based upon reading readiness levels. This is important. You are teaching the skill. If the reading is too difficult, the student will not be able to master the skill. English learners will need support. This might be another student, a graphic organizer, sentence frames for expressing ideas, or text in their first language. It is dependent upon their level. This is an example of planning for differentiation. Students will receive verbal feedback as they work. This will be a formative assessment because I will monitor students as they work and provide immediate corrective feedback if necessary. I could also stretch those writers who are ready for a challenge.

Writing: Focus on topic sentences and the connections to the main idea. Model with the reading example from the morning and demonstrate writing a topic sentence. Introduce the graphic organizer (figure 2.2) to determine important supporting facts. I will use the I Do, We Do, You Do (Fisher & Frey, 2008) structure to help students understand how to choose the best details. This is an area where I know students struggle. They will want to include all the details, and they need to be taught to discern which details are the most important. I will concentrate on the I Do and We Do today. During the We Do, we will use one of the passages read by students this morning. As a class, we will determine important understandings and how the text supports our conclusions. The conclusion is there, but it will not be addressed today.

I Do, We Do, You Do (Fisher & Frey, 2008) is a gradual release model of instruction. The I Do portion is the modeling for the students. The teacher is doing the work and thinking aloud for students. The students are actively listening and taking notes. The We Do portion is a guided practice of the skill. Students are involved but are not working independently. They are interacting with the teacher by asking and answering questions. The teacher is guiding the work. They may be in front of the class or overseeing a group working on the task. The You Do portion allows the students to do the work independently and take responsibility for the outcome. This is the work that will act as a formative assessment of understanding. This work will provide the opportunity for feedback. That feedback can be written or verbal, but it is specific and focused upon the standard being addressed.

Day 2

Students will get more practice with the skills taught the day before. Partner structure will be used for both reading and writing. At the end of the day, the partners will complete a graphic organizer (figure 2.2), without a conclusion, with a new reading. This lets me see if they are applying the process to the reading because it is new to them. It is not something that we have previously discussed. This gives the opportunity for the students to apply their learning and for me to see where they are missing the mark. Written and oral feedback will be given regarding main idea and details. I am only focusing on pulling out the main idea and details to determine if they are able to do this. I will be monitoring the discussions and providing verbal feedback in the form of questions to help students move on if they get stuck. I will have questions such as: Why do you think that is the main idea? What evidence do you have? Why is that a good detail to support the main idea? You want to avoid yes and no questions. Students need to explain their thinking in order for me to diagnose the problem. The more they give me, the better I can determine their problem. Questions for this purpose should be open ended.

The subsequent days will involve reinforcing and teaching the components. As the days progress, it is likely that a new grouping will be necessary. Some students will be mastering the ideas and others will need remediation. That is all part of effective differentiation, which will be covered in depth in chapter 7.

The organizer in figure 2.2 allows you to take a quick inventory of students who are mastering the focus standards and those who are not. It serves as the formative assessment. Remember that it is a holistic look and you are not marking the work for a grade. This work is to provide information about the student understanding and the possible gaps in understanding. From this work, a plan of differentiation would be easy to determine. For instance, the first box will allow me to see if the students can determine the main idea and craft a topic sentence that clearly expressed the idea. If they cannot, that is where I will begin, and I can more effectively group students to help them master the skill. The organizer provides me the ability to give students effective and specific feedback on one or more components of the final piece. That feedback is what the students can use to move their work to the next level. Start with what the student needs most, and tackle each component separately. Resist the marking up of the whole document. That is defeating for the students. They cannot work on everything at once. Chunk the work for them so that it is manageable, and they will persevere with support.

Main Idea/Topic	
Sentence:	
Understanding	Support (from text)
Understanding	Support (from text)
Understanding	Support (from text)
Conclusion:	
Sentence:	

Figure 2.2. Graphic Organizer.

CONCLUSION

It is critical to engage in effective short- and long-term planning. That planning should be based upon the most essential learning that needs to occur throughout the school year. It is imperative to remain flexible and adjust the learning and the pacing for the students based on the results of formative assessments aligned to the standards. It is not about keeping the pace based on an arbitrary pacing guide, even one created by the teachers. The pace of the learning in the class is determined by the students and adjusted by the teacher based on formative assessments. Differentiation is a part of the planning process. Pedagogy is a part of the plan as well. Effective pedagogy must be used to achieve the goals. What you will teach and how you will teach it are both considered in the planning process. Without clear planning, it is easy to get off track and not accomplish the goals of a unit, which results in time wasted. We do not have time to waste in a classroom. Every moment is precious!

Try It: In groups of three or four, develop a unit of study that will span several weeks. Determine the essential and highly desirable standards that will be focused upon for that unit. Remember, these are the standards that you will assess throughout the learning. Also, create a plan of when you will focus upon each of the standards. We will continue working with the plan and the standards in the following chapters.

Chapter Three

Lesson Design

Lesson designing is the process of thinking through the how of teaching. What will you do to make sure that the students reach mastery of the standards you are focusing on for this learning segment? It is where you will demonstrate the ability to think through the standards and create an assessment that is aligned to the standard at the right level of rigor. It is also where you will think through how you will support specific groups of students. You should be considering those on grade level, those above, and those who need scaffolding and support of some sort. How might you differentiate the learning in order to help the students reach the level of mastery? The scaffolding that you will provide for their learning will be based on the results of your pretest because the analysis of that pretest will help you see what skills need supporting.

At the beginning of a teaching career, or when you are trying to adopt this new paradigm, it is best to be very explicit about the planning process. It is the support for the thinking that will eventually become second nature. Before you rode a two-wheel bicycle, you had training wheels. Think of a lesson plan in that fashion. It is providing a structure for success. While it may seem to be tedious, in the long run the planning and the process will help make you more effective at planning.

The lesson plan I am sharing with you in this chapter is one that I use with my student teachers. Because they will graduate with a credential that states they are prepared to teach English learners, they must be able to demonstrate that they can effectively support English learners in all of their lessons. In addition, they must be thinking about how they will differentiate in the guided practice portion of the lesson. How exactly have you differentiated the content, process, or product for the learners? Differentiation in learning will be addressed in more detail in later chapters. While the plan is presented in a linear fashion on paper so it is more easily followed, it should not be created in a linear fashion. There should be a system to the planning in order to keep the lesson focused and clear.

OBJECTIVES, STANDARDS, AND ASSESSMENT

All learning begins with determining what will be done at the end of the lesson. What will students be required to know? How will they demonstrate what they know? The questions have to be clearly answered before planning the learning experiences. This is the Backward Design supported by the work of Wiggins and McTighe (2005). They recommend the following steps: identify the desired results, identify the acceptable evidence, and then design the learning opportunities. That is why I have lumped these three items together. This "beginning with the end in mind" is a Stephen Covey (1989) principle. Successful people know where they are going, which takes planning. It is no different in teaching. Teachers need to know what they want students to be able to do and then build a plan to get them there. That plan should also include some ideas of how you might deal with obstacles that might occur.

This relates to the learning from previous chapters. The short-term and long-term plans will guide the work of lesson planning. Think of it as a funnel. A team will begin the planning by taking a broad look at the year and determining those essential and highly desirable standards they will cover and assess. Then, they will narrow that down to months and weeks. Next, it is time to plan the actual learning experiences, which is when the lesson plan comes into play. The first step is to have a clear objective and then share it with the students. It helps to frame exactly what is expected as a result of the teaching and practice. It should also clearly align with the standard and reflect work at the proper level of rigor. In order to do that, you must be unpacking the standard and creating the assessment to match. In fact, the objectives, standards, and assessment piece should be done at the same time. This will ensure that they are aligned and actually measure what you want to measure.

Figures 3.1 and 3.2 will help with the planning of individual lessons for any unit. Each of the components will be fully discussed in the chapter. The questions provided at the end will help to self-evaluate the work when it is completed.

Again, let us consider those essential and highly desirable standards from the last chapter. All of these would be a part of the unit planned for two weeks. It will be important to have formative assessments as a part of the plan so students will receive feedback and improve over the course of the instruction.

CCSS.ELA-Literacy.W.4.4

Lesson Plan		
Subject		Date
Standards	Clearly linked to the lesson objectives Included by number and description Appropriate for the instruction	
Objectives	Learning targets are clearly stated in clear assessable performance terms. The objectives must be clearly aligned with the standards and the assessment. The assessment must actually measure what it purports to measure.	
Materials (visuals, supplementary)	Describes all materials used including technology.	
Introduction (Connect to prior learning)	Provides a clear introduction and relation to prior knowledge. Also includes engagement strategies that will involve the students. The introduction is your chance to excite the students about what they will learn.	
Procedures/Teaching (Comprehensible input, interaction and engagement)	Provides enough detail so that a competent substitute would be able to follow the plan and be successful with teaching it the way you envision. Chosen instructional activity supports learning objectives and provides for student engagement with the material. The strategy is applied correctly. The instructional strategy will lead to the learning being assessed. The presentation is logical and sequenced for learning.	
Procedures/Differentiation: Small Group Instruction (Meaningful activities, strategies, interaction) Should include modifications to <u>process, content or product</u>.	Above Level: Demonstrates thoughtful inclusion of activities or material for learners who need to move beyond the material. The strategies and activities are clearly explained and appropriate. They will result in a more challenging or deeper involvement with the material.	
	On Level: Demonstrates thoughtful inclusion of activities or material for learners who are on grade level. The strategies and activities are clearly explained and appropriate. The students will get solid practice with the content and will produce something that demonstrates they understand the content.	
	Below Level: Demonstrates thoughtful inclusion of activities or material for learners who are in need of support to learn the content objectives. The strategies and activities are clearly explained and appropriate. The students are given support, but the content is not reduced in simplicity.	
	ELL : Demonstrates thoughtful inclusion of activities or material for learners who are in need of language support in order to master the content. The strategies and activities are clearly explained and appropriate.	
Accommodations & Modifications	If there is no small group work in the lesson, the modifications for learners need to be explained clearly here. How will you support the learners listed above in the lesson? Are there students with specific needs (IEP)?	

Figure 3.1. Lesson Plan Template.

Produce clear and coherent writing in which the development and organization are appropriate to task, purpose, and audience.

CCSS.ELA-Literacy.W.4.1.a

Introduce a topic or text clearly, state an opinion, and create an organizational structure in which related ideas are grouped to support the writer's purpose.

CCSS.ELA-Literacy.W.4.1.b

Provide reasons that are supported by facts and details.

CCSS.ELA-Literacy.W.4.1.d

Provide a concluding statement or section related to the opinion presented.

The unit will begin with a pretest that is written to align with the final goal. The pretest would be an extended response item that requires students to read, or be read, a story that they could then respond to in writing. It should state, as a part of the directions, that the students must include their opinion and support it with examples from the story. This would enable the teacher to

Closure	Brings lesson to a closure with an activity that reinforces the learning or gives students an opportunity to express understanding or questions.
Assessment	Clearly linked to the objectives and standards Allows for assessment of all students There is a clear understanding of proficiency (rubric, scoring guide,)
Lesson Self-Evaluation (Cite specific examples of the areas you focus on in your reflection.)	• From the beginning to the end I was **intentional** in every aspect of my lesson. • My lesson objectives were clear to me **and** to the students. • I provided an engaging introduction to the lesson to stimulate my students' attention and provided focus to the lesson content. • I considered engagement and formative assessment before the lesson. • The lesson content was aligned with the standards and was appropriate for the needs of my students. • The instructional strategies I chose were effective for the lesson content. • I consciously and actively involved **all** my students in the lesson, addressing differentiation, inclusion, and diversity issues. • I employed higher level questioning that encouraged students' cognitive processing. • I exhibited positive and effective classroom management throughout the lesson. • I provided a clear lesson closure. • I included a means for accurately assessing the student's learning of the content. • I have evidence of student learning.

Figure 3.2.   Lesson Plan Template, continued.

determine if the students can produce the clear and coherent writing the standard demands. All of the elements like a topic sentence and a concluding sentence could also be evaluated so that the teacher could target the needs of the students. The writing they produce will enable the teacher to see the strengths and the gaps of the students in relation to the specific standards, which makes the assessment meaningful to the instruction that will follow. The full creation of an aligned assessment piece will be covered in chapter 4.

OBJECTIVES

Any good lesson plan begins with an objective. Objectives or goals should be specific, measurable, attainable, aligned to the standard, focused on results, and time bound (Doran, 1981). The goals should clearly state what students will be able to do and when. They should clearly be aligned to the standard and focused on achieving the desired results in a specific amount of time. If the learning objective is not clear to the students, they might think that the goal of the learning is to complete an activity (Chappuis, 2012). A final objective for the learning of this unit might be as follows: *As a result of this writing unit, students will be able to independently produce, at a proficient level, a clear and coherent response to literature, which contains a clearly stated opinion, details that support their ideas, and an effective topic and concluding sentence.*

This goal is tied directly to the standards that make up the unit and is very specific about what will make up the response. It is a grade-level standard and is attainable for the students with the proper support. All of the components are easily measured with a rubric, and it clearly states the performance level expectation. The creation of this rubric will be discussed in the following chapter. The rubric will enable specific feedback to be given to the students so they can make improvements to their writing. This objective is also time bound because the unit will end in two weeks, which is the inferred time for this objective. That is the final goal for the unit, but each of the lessons will have a building block objective to get to that point.

After the pretest, the lessons would begin with the building blocks to the successful final writing. If most of the class was not able to write an effective topic sentence, that is a logical beginning point. The topic sentence might be something some have control over. However, since it changes depending on the genre, it would probably be the starting point. The objective, then, for the first lesson or two might be the following: *At the end of two work sessions, the students will be able to use a graphic organizer and peer support to help them determine a theme and create a proficient level topic sentence as measured by the grade-level writing rubric.*

Again the objective meets all of the criteria: specific, measurable, attainable, directly aligned to the standard, result focused, and time bound. Now that I am clear about what I want the students to be able to do after two work sessions, I can plan how I will get them there. I need to think through the procedures and how I will teach writing a topic sentence. What steps must be taken to write an effective topic sentence? How will I need to support students? The answers to these two questions will result in my procedures and teaching.

PROCEDURES/TEACHING

I will be writing this in a Think Aloud fashion again. I want to make the thinking behind the planning as clear as I can. While student teachers will need to complete detailed lesson plans, practicing teachers might not need to go through this process in depth. However, if you are a practicing teacher and are being observed, this would be a great structure to present to your administrator. They would certainly be able to see that you have thought through the lesson when you present this lesson plan to them.

For the two lessons, I will concentrate only on the writing of the topic sentence. I might have a graphic organizer that contains all of the portions of the finished product. For this particular lesson, the students will not complete the whole organizer. I would only have them complete the part that pertains to a topic sentence. I would choose the organizer that best suits my overall purpose, and I might even consider using multiple organizers depending upon the support needed. I need to give students more than one opportunity to practice determining the theme or topic and writing a topic sentence. I will also have to be able to provide feedback to all of the students so they are able to fix any errors occurring, which means I will have to organize them so that I am able to provide that in a reasonably quick fashion. Feedback must be immediate and specific so that students will be able to see what they need to keep working on (Chappuis, 2012). I know that I have to be able to set aside time for this because it is critical that they receive the feedback and act upon it.

I need to first introduce the idea of a topic sentence for a response to literature to the students. This will relate to other work we have done, but the genre is different and the purpose of the topic sentence is different as well. This will be best done in a whole group. Depending upon the grade level, I would arrange the students so that I could monitor engagement and use partner talk as a structure. I will have two examples of good sentences and two of poor sentences. They will clearly identify the theme, and I will be explicit about pointing this out. I will model thinking about the first two examples and then involve them on the second pair. I will use a partner talk structure so that all are involved in the discussion. This will help them talk about why the sentences are well written or not. I will then use a guided practice format to lead the students in the creation of a topic sentence about our class reading from last week. We will determine the theme and write a topic sentence to begin a response to literature essay. I will end the session with a formative assessment using white boards. I will put a sentence up and have them rate it using 1 for no and 2 for yes. I will use three sentences based on familiar stories so the students will have some context. This will help me determine those who do not understand, and I will be able to work with them independently if needed. I will also use the results to partner the students for their task.

PROCEDURES/DIFFERENTIATION

For differentiation, I need to consider the makeup of my class. I need to support some students to reach the proficient level. All have the graphic organizer, but some might also need other supports like a word bank or a sentence frame. In order to be ready to support them, I need to have thought about what they will need and how it would be best presented to them. For the purposes of the planning, I will consider above level, on level, below level, and English learners as I differentiate.

Above Level

I know that some students will be able to write a topic sentence without much difficulty. For them, I want to use the expectations for the highest level in the rubric. I would be structuring the work so that they will be able to score above proficiency for the grade level. In this case, they may not use the sentence frame that will be provided to others. I would want their topic sentence to be originally stated and engaging. While other students will be working in partners, I will have this group work independently. They do not really need the support. I will have to take a minute or two to explain what I want to see from them. I would begin by sharing the rubric language, which will help them see what they are trying to accomplish. I also want to have an example already written for the examples I used earlier. Their task might be to come up with an original topic sentence for something they have read and also to correct the ones that we rated poor in our lesson. I would then have an enrichment activity they could engage in when finished. They will likely finish earlier than the others. I have to be ready for this so they will not be asking what to do next. The enrichment task I provide might be related directly to this activity, or it could be related to other work. Many times students who are proficient are asked to help others. While that is a good use of their time sometimes, I think it is often overused. Having them work with others does promote many socialization and collaboration skills, but it can also result in boredom for the advanced students and overreliance for those needing help. Sometimes well-meaning students do the work for others rather than encouraging them to work through obstacles. I, as the teacher, want to be the one to coach those who need the most help. I will provide written feedback to the students and may conference individually with them after reviewing their work.

On Level

Many of the students are ready to attempt this task on their own or with a partner. They have the graphic organizer to complete. I will have them work in partners so that they can discuss as we did in the lesson. This gives me the opportunity to use their discussions as formative assessment and provide feedback or questions that will help them think about the work. It also helps me because I can talk to two students at once, increasing the likelihood of interacting with all students during the work session. Why do you think that is the theme? What evidence do you have? Those questions will let me see if they are using the text and also prepare them for the next steps in the process. While I will not prohibit them from using the sentence frame, I will also require that they rewrite the sentence using other language. This supports them reaching proficiency but will also help them possibly reach the highest level on the rubric. If they finish the task early, they can rewrite one or both of the poor examples from the earlier lesson. That will be done independently. This way, they have been supported in the learning and the independent work acts as a formative assessment for me. As they work, I will monitor and provide feedback. I will also provide written feedback on the independent work they complete.

Below Level

A few of my students may be at a level where they are unable to craft a complete sentence without support. For this group, I will provide a specific sentence frame. In the story _____, the author teaches the reader about _____ by _____. The students will be able to complete the frame resulting in a sentence that will introduce their work clearly. I will model using this with a book we have all read. The following is a possible completed sentence: In the story *Charlotte's Web*, the author teaches the reader about friendship by introducing us to a group of animals from a farm that become friends and help one another. I will also support the students with the class word bank. This will allow them to retrieve words more easily and not get stuck in the writing. I will let them work in partners to write a topic sentence for a book they have read.

English Learners

Since English learners could be at one of five levels of proficiency, the support would depend upon the level. The sentence frames and the word bank would certainly act as supports for many of the levels. However, English learners may also need support in their first language to even make sense of the task. That support should be offered if it is needed. If the student struggles with writing, they may need to respond verbally. A good first step for this student, then, would be to express the topic sentence verbally rather than in writing. It also is impacted by the supports available at the school. Many schools have bilingual aides who can work with small groups of students needing that support. The considerations are vast and need to be determined by the teacher's knowledge of the students.

ACCOMMODATIONS/MODIFICATIONS

This is where I would explicitly think about those modifications that specific students need. Maybe there are students who get more time or have a special accommodation due to an Individualized Education Plan (IEP). That information should be shared here. That support needs to be thought about beforehand so that all the required materials are there to be used by the student. It may necessitate that a support staff member be there, and the schedule must permit that support.

CLOSURE

As a closure, I will have partner teams join together into groups of four and share their sentences. This way they are hearing more examples. These will be mixed levels, but all will have an example to share. By putting them into groups and having them share, they all get the chance to share, and I will only need about 3–5 minutes. If everyone was to share, it would take considerably longer; students would lose interest, which might lead to behavior issues. I will have them all turn in their work so that I can provide written feedback or conference with them if needed.

ASSESSMENT

A variety of assessments are used in this lesson. I am using it in the introduction to group students. The quick white board response will help me know who gets it and who does not. I am also using their discussions and work as an assessment. It will allow me to provide immediate feedback to groups at least once in the work session. Because most of the class is in partners, I will be able to see everyone. It would be considerably more difficult to see all if they were all working individually. After I have reviewed the work from the day, I would provide written feedback or work with students in a writing conference to address errors. I would be able to strategically group students for the writing conferences. Putting students with similar errors together would enable me to address the issues and not be overwhelmed with individual conferences.

REFLECTION

I will not go over each of the reflection questions, but it would be wise to think about how the plan supports the learning. It would also be wise to think about the evidence of success for the lesson. How do I know the students learned what I wanted them to learn? If they did not, what will I do next? When students do not do well with a lesson, it does not mean that the teacher is at fault and not effective. It means that the students were not able to grasp it the way it was taught. The sign of a bad teacher is one who does nothing about students not doing well and simply moves on to the next lesson. That is not an option.

Lesson Plan

Subject	Wrting		Date	
Objectives	At the end of two work sessions, the student will be able to use a graphic organizer and peer support to help them determine a theme and create a proficient level topic sentence as measured by the grade level writing rubric.			
Standards	CCSS.ELA-Literacy.W.4.1.a Introduce a topic or text clearly, state an opinion, and create an organizational structure in which related ideas are grouped to support the writer's purpose.			
Materials (visuals, supplementary)	Chart paper with sample topic sentences (two well written, two poorly written)			
Introduction (Connect to prior learning)	I will talk to the students about the personal narrative they wrote last month. I will remind them about how we wanted people to be eager to read our work so we made the first sentence our hook. I will then share 3 of the best topic sentences and we will discuss what made them good examples.			
Procedures (Comprehensible input, interaction and engagement)	I will introduce the idea of a topic sentence for a response to literature to the students. This will be best done in a whole group. I will arrange the students so they can all see the board. I will have two examples of good sentences and two of poor sentences written on the board. I will model thinking about the first two and then involve them on the second pair. I will use a partner talk structure so that are involved in the discussion. This will help them talk about why the sentences are well written or not. I will then use a guided practice format to lead the students in the creation of a topic sentence about our class reading from last week. We will determine the theme and write a topic sentence to begin a response to literature essay. I will end the session with a formative assessment using white boards. I will put a sentence up and have them rate it using 1 for no and 2 for yes. I will use three sentences based on familiar stories so the student will have some context. This will help me see those who are not understanding and I will be able to work with them independently if needed. I will also use the results to partner the students for their task. (formative assessment)			
Procedures: Small Group Instruction (Meaningful activities, strategies, interaction)	**Above Level:** Students will work independently rather than in partners. They will be asked to rewrite the poor examples from the lesson as well as to create an original topic sentence for a book they have read. When they finish, they will be asked to find three supporting details for their identified theme and to complete the rest of the graphic organizer.			
	On Level: Students will be strategically paired based on the results of the white board quiz. They will be asked to create a topic sentence for a book they have both read (one of our stories from the year). They will then be asked to independently rewrite the two poor examples to make them better. They can compare their sentences after they have finished and then together create a new version based on their individual work.			
	Below Level: Students will be grouped in pairs or a small group and be guided by the teacher. They will be provided a sentence frame to help them craft a sentence. In the story _____, the author teaches the reader about _____ by _____. I will use the following as an example for them: In the story Charlotte's Web, the author teaches the reader about friendship by sharing a story about a group of animals from a farm who become friends and help one another.			
	ELL : In addition to the frame, they will be provided a word bank. If the student is a level 1 or 2, they will be able to express the sentence verbally rather than in writing. The teacher or aide will then act as the scribe for the student.			

Figure 3.3. Completed Lesson Plan.

Accommodations & Modifications	This is where you would explicitly think about those modifications that specific students get. Maybe there are students that get more time or have a special accommodation due to an Individualized Education Plan (IEP). That information should be shared here.
Closure	Students, in groups of four, will share their sentences with one another verbally. This will be a two minute share.
Assessment	Formative assessment will be used throughout. I will be monitoring the work and asking guiding questions. I will also have all students turn in their work so that they may receive written feedback or feedback through conferencing the following day.

Figure 3.4. Completed Lesson Plan, continued.

I know the thinking aloud made it seem that the lesson plan would be exhaustive. Figures 3.3 and 3.4 demonstrate an example of a completed plan. For my beginning teachers, I always ask that they put down enough information so that a qualified substitute could teach the lesson. This process takes a little time starting out, but then it becomes the way of thinking and the process streamlines. In order to achieve that change in thinking, the structure of the lesson plan is essential at the beginning. Think of the lesson plan as the structure that will enable you to teach more effectively for all learners because it forces you to consider them before teaching.

In order to know if the lesson was effective, students must be given the opportunity to show what they understand. The assessment pieces will help determine the level of student understanding. That is why they must be carefully crafted and aligned closely with the objectives and standards. In the next chapter, we will look at crafting assessment pieces for the unit that will help move the instruction along.

Try It: Together with a partner, use the lesson plan template and prepare a lesson for one of the following Indiana 3rd grade ELA Informational Text standards. If you prefer to use your own state standards or the Common Core standards here, feel free. Make the process meaningful for you. I am not advocating for any particular standards here; they simply define the goal. After you have finished, switch your work with another partner group and provide feedback on the lesson.

RI.1: Ask and answer questions to demonstrate understanding of a text, referring explicitly to the text as the basis for the answers.

RI.2: Determine the main idea of a text; recount the key details and explain how they support the main idea.

RI.7: Use information gained from illustrations (e.g., maps, photographs) and the words in a text to demonstrate understanding of the text (e.g., where, when, why, and how key events occur).

- Does it clearly demonstrate support/engagement for a variety of learners?
- Is the work aligned to the standards?
- Is it likely to produce work that will be able to help the teacher move the learning forward?
- What might you change? Why?

Subject/Grade		Date	
Objectives			
Standards-			
Materials (visuals, supplementary)			
Introduction (Connect to prior learning)			
Procedures (Comprehensible input, interaction and engagement)			
Procedures: Small Group Instruction (Meaningful activities, strategies, interaction)	Above Level:		
	On Level:		
	Below Level:		
	ELL :		
Accommodations & Modifications			
Closure			
Assessment			
Lesson Self-Evaluation			

Figure 3.5. Lesson Plan Template Copy.

Chapter Four

Assessment Item Formats

In chapters 2 and 3, we looked at the planning that must occur in order to keep the learning on track and paced appropriately. Chapter 3 focused on creating lesson plans that matched the objectives. We must now consider taking those objectives and writing assessment questions that will enable us to monitor student learning as a part of the unit. The assessment questions need to be based upon the standards and give the students the opportunity to provide clear evidence of their understanding. They must include the right questions and be in a format that enables good analysis of understanding. If the question does not provide a glimpse into the thinking and ability of the student, it will not yield enough information to make instructional decisions. Making appropriate instructional decisions is always the ultimate objective of formative assessments.

In order to determine the best question format, let's look at the different kinds of questions that can make up an assessment. Every kind of question has a place and a purpose. It is important to use the right kind of question to yield the information needed.

SELECTED RESPONSE

Selected response questions are in a format that allows students to choose from a list of possible answers. The four types of selected response questions are as follows: multiple choice, binary choice, matching, and fill in the blank. They can be effective, but there are a few guidelines for writing good selected response questions (Ainsworth, Kamm, Peery, Pitchford, & Rose, 2011).

First of all, the question should clearly match the standard. In order to do this, time must be taken to "unwrap the standard" (Ainsworth, 2003, p. 1) and determine what it is exactly the student must know and be able to do. There has to be a clear consensus on this, and the item must match the rigor in the standard. Ainsworth (2003) suggests looking at the nouns and the verbs contained in the standard and matching them to Bloom's Taxonomy. The process helps to make sure that the question is not on the recall level when it should be asking the student to evaluate something. Many selected response questions are written at that recall level and do not challenge the students or ask that they apply their learning, which is not helpful for analysis. It is important to write selected response questions so they reflect higher-order thinking and not simply recall of information. A question focused on recall does not help you know what a student understands. If the standard is simply asking that they recall information that is fine, but that is rarely the case. If the standard requires more, the questions must be crafted so that the students can demonstrate the highest level of the standard.

Another consideration is that the questions need to be based partly on new material (Ainsworth, 2003). For example, if you are working with interpreting graphs in math, the questions should contain graphs that have never been used with the students. They should have to use what they have learned and make sense of the new graph on their own. Having them evaluate a new situation will enable the teacher to determine if there is a problem in the students' thought processes. The other possible answer choices should be representative of answers that will result when they misapply the process. Being able to clearly define the issue involved in any misunderstanding will aid in the development of a remediation plan.

Finally, the questions should be brief and clear. It is not about trying to trick the student. They should not have to figure out what you are trying to ask (Stiggins, 1997). The questions should not contain clues to the answer, complex phrasing, ambiguous statements, or difficult vocabulary (Ainsworth et al., 2011). We have all taken tests where we could not figure out the question. The language was confusing. That is not the point of an assessment. We want to know what the students know. Keep it simple.

Multiple Choice

Generally there are four choices and they are labeled A, B, C, and D or 1, 2, 3, and 4. Many standardized tests are written in this format. Many of the tests that are included in textbook adoptions have this kind of test. I am not advocating that you not use them, but be careful about how they are written. Make sure they will yield some information for you and they are not simply for recall of information. If you must use prewritten tests, you can simply include a requirement that a student explain why the answer they chose is the best answer. That short explanation will help you glimpse their thinking. I used to tell my students to put their thinking on the page. That is what the write-up will allow them to do.

One benefit of this format is it is easy to grade and can easily be put into a data system that will allow line item analysis. Many schools use this kind of system. However, if the questions are poorly written, the analysis does not offer a true understanding of the misconceptions. The short response can be looked at and evaluated using a holistic rubric and then be put into a data system. That would provide more information because the rubric language would be descriptive enough to determine some misconceptions.

Multiple Choice Examples

All questions should have a best answer not just a correct answer. It should require some evaluation. Having the best answer, not just one correct answer, allows for you to write items with choices that require thought on the part of the student. They cannot simply eliminate answers. They have to evaluate each answer, which brings in higher-order thinking skills.

At the end of the story *Charlotte's Web*, why does Wilbur want to keep the egg sac?

   a. It belonged to his good friend Charlotte.
   b. He is keeping his promise to his friend.
   c. He wants to keep it safe and dry.
   d. He wants Fern to be able to see it.

Out of all of the possible choices here, the best answer is B. His main motivator is his loyalty to his friend and keeping the promise made. It is important to him that it was Charlotte's, and he also wants to keep it safe. However, he wants those things out of loyalty to a friend.

Questions must assess the target skills. All questions must be assessing the standard at the proper level of rigor. The above question is not a recall question. It is asking students to think about the story and analyze the motivation of the characters. That analysis results in a higher level of rigor.

The questions should be written clearly and without clues to the answer. It is important to write incomplete statement items so that there is not a clue to the right choice (Popham, 2003). This is often a grammatical clue: One example of a reptile is an A. frog, B. salamander, C. spider, or D. alligator. The only choice that completes the sentence correctly is alligator. This can be avoided by removing "an" at the end of the phrase (One example of a reptile is).

The answers should contain plausible distractors that reflect common misunderstandings and do not include humor.

Which step would follow collection in the water cycle?

    a. Precipitation
    b. Condensation
    c. Evaporation
    d. Recycle

In the example, answers A, B, and C are all parts of the cycle. C is the correct answer because A precedes the collection and B comes after the evaporation. The idea of recycling is not a part of the cycle and should not be a part of the question. It is an automatic elimination.

Binary Choice

A binary choice item provides students with two possible choices. They are generally True/False or Yes/No; however, they can be labeled in other ways as well. Just about any comparative set of terms can be used for the answers. A few possibilities include: correct/incorrect, plausible/implausible, possible/impossible, and accurate/inaccurate. You may want to carefully choose the language to get students thinking in a variety of ways. True and false requires a different kind of thinking than determining if something is plausible, for example. True and false is more of a recall situation and determining plausibility might require comparative analysis. The terms used to define the choices can immediately raise the rigor of the question.

Binary choice items are excellent to determine if students have committed facts to memory. However, it is important not to overuse them. The use of items like this promotes the memorization of facts. That is not all we want. There are facts that students should be able to recall that might help in the higher-level thinking. It is important to know if they have that recall. Use these kinds of selected response questions for the right purposes.

Binary Choice Guidelines

Popham (2003) suggests that binary choice questions be written in pairs, not singly. This is a time-saving device for you as the test writer. If there is a positive statement about certain content, there should also be a negative. You should not put them both on the same test; one can remain in your test bank ready for another assessment in the future. If you are giving multiple formative assessments over the content, you will want to shift the questions so students have to read carefully. Phrase them so that items must be read carefully. This is not to trick the student, it is to prevent them skimming through the test. We want them to think.

The question should also only involve one concept. It should be clearly false or clearly true, not "sort of." Below is an example for consideration.

Today's pitchers throw the ball at a much higher speed than in the past because they have better coaching. (possibly)

This question is supposing that the pitching speeds have increased specifically due to coaching. That could be sort of true, but it is probably not the only reason. The equipment may also be a factor in the increase of speed. It might even be debated that some pitchers in the past might have pitched just as fast, but were not accurately measured. This is not clearly true or false.

Popham (2003) also recommends that the items be of equal length and that the test not be lopsided. It should not be predominantly true or false. There should be a balance between the two.

Matching

Matching items require two lists of words or phrases that have some sort of association. They are similar to binary choice in that you can cover a good deal of content with one question. Items like this are good for low-level skills like memorization. If you want to make sure that they are able to recognize examples, this is the test item to use. Consider the following example.

Directions: On the line next to each description in column A print the letter of the person in column B who is most associated with the description. Each name in column B can be used only once.

Column A	Column B
__1. Signed the Civil Rights Act	A. Medgar Evers
__2. Lawyer in *Brown v. Board of Education*	B. Ernest Green
__3. Advocated peaceful solutions	C. Lyndon Johnson
__4. Participated in the Woolworth sit-in	D. Martin Luther King Jr.
__5. One of the Little Rock Nine	E. Thurgood Marshall
	F. Franklin McCain

Matching items should be short and to the point. There should not be copious reading. It is also important to make sure that all the items are related to one concept. In the example, the concept is the civil rights movement and the choices make sense. Nothing is glaringly out of place. If I had included a name like Benjamin Franklin, it would have been a clue to eliminate that choice. All of the choices are people involved in the civil rights movement.

   An important consideration is that there should always be more choices than available answer spaces (Popham, 2003). This way, students have to evaluate the answers and cannot simply eliminate a few and then guess at the others. Also, have a logical way to display the choices. Do not be random. In the above example, I have listed them alphabetically. It does not provide any clue as to the placement of the answers (answers C, E, D, F, B).

Fill in the Blank

Just like the matching, the fill-in-the-blank choice questions generally have a word bank. Again, like the matching, there should be more choices than blanks for the answers. There should only be one blank per item, and do not make the length of the blank a clue to the word that fits. The blanks need to be the same size. You do not want the size to indicate the word that fills the space. One solution is to use numbers or letters for the choices and the student can simply place the corresponding letter or number into the sentence.

While selected response questions have their place in the world of assessment, they are sometimes not the best choice because they will not yield enough information to make a determination about student understanding. Without careful thought about the creation of the questions, they can focus too much on isolated facts. That is not what we want to stress to students. We want them to be able to think and to apply their learning. Our questions have to reflect that desire. Selected response questions are great for certain applications, but do not work in all. For instance, selected response questions do not clearly demonstrate an ability to write. Students may be able to choose a grammatically correct sentence, but the focus in writing should be on the creation of the sentence. A selected response test will not measure that effectively. The point of assessment, remember, is to know what the student understands. If you want to know how students might apply knowledge or how they can compare and contrast a topic, you will need to let them write about it. For that we need to give students the opportunity to write.

This brings us to another form of assessment, the constructed response. This can be a short response or an extended response. This format allows the evaluation of the content as well as the expression of that content. Constructed response questions can be written in two basic forms: short answer and extended response. They allow the students to express their understanding in an abbreviated fashion or a lengthy response (Popham, 2003).

SHORT ANSWER

A short answer question can be a fill in the blank without answer choices, a single sentence response, or a problem in math. The point is that it is short and targeted. For instance, after a lesson on nouns and verbs I might ask the students to identify the noun and verb in a random sentence. I could put that sentence on the board or have a variety of sentences and pass them out randomly. I could have them produce a sentence to check on their ability to write a sentence with certain criteria. They would have to produce one or two sentences. For instance, I may want them to use a parenthetical phrase. In that case, they only produce one sentence using a parenthetical phrase. I can also use this format to test the ability of students to grasp the main idea of a piece of writing. I simply ask that they express, in one or two sentences, the main idea of the passage. It is quick and to the point. It is a short assessment that can occur quickly at the end of a lesson. This is a great way to wrap up a lesson. The results will lead to the next step with the students in the class. In the previous chapter, the lesson plan focused on the writing of a topic sentence. The work the students created independently could have served as a short response assessment. They were not writing the whole essay, just a component of the essay.

EXTENDED RESPONSE

The extended response is just as it sounds: it requires a more thoughtful response. It is used when a single sentence or short response will not suffice. This is the dreaded essay question. You might have dreaded them as a student, but as a teacher, they will help you diagnose the thinking of a student. They provide the opportunity for integration of ideas. They are higher-level questions that demand students critically think about the topic. For instance, a teacher might ask students to recall two causes that led to the Civil War, then ask that they choose one and explain how each side saw the issue. Students might also be asked to choose a side in the war and defend their side with facts from the reading. This would require a lengthy response and would clearly demonstrate if the student is making clear connections about content.

While selected response questions require a key to grade, the constructed response questions require a rubric (Ainsworth, 2003). A rubric will clearly spell out what is required in the response. The language used in the development of the guide must be specific. It also must state criteria that are measurable and observable. Finally, it must be tied to the task directions and the rigor of the standard.

For the purposes of examples here, I am referring back to the standards used in chapter 2 to construct scoring guides for both types of essay questions.

CCSS.ELA-Literacy.W.4.1.a

Introduce a topic or text clearly, state an opinion, and create an organizational structure in which related ideas are grouped to support the writer's purpose.

CCSS.ELA-Literacy.W.4.1.b

Provide reasons that are supported by facts and details.

CCSS.ELA-Literacy.W.4.1.d

Provide a concluding statement or section related to the opinion presented.

CREATING RUBRICS

The rubrics in tables 4.1 and 4.2 were created to evaluate a product, in this case, some writing. Rubrics can be created for an end product or the process of learning. The only kind of situation where a rubric does not work well is one where there is only one correct answer. If something is either right or wrong, you would not use a rubric. Rubrics provide a structure for observations and conclusions about student learning. Using the rubric and matching the observations with descriptions of performance help avert judging. It is not about your opinion; it is about meeting the desired level of performance described in the rubric.

If you were planning to evaluate a process such as the acquiring of physical skills like dribbling, shooting, batting, the use of lab equipment, presentation skills, or cooperative behaviors, a rubric focused on the process would help provide feedback (Brookhart, 2013). The rubric would have to include the correct elements of that process. For instance, in batting you would want to include stance, grip, follow-through, and timing. That would enable specific feedback about what the person controlled and what he or she needed to work on to gain proficiency.

It is common to see a rubric used for a product at the end of a unit. This might be a paper, a structured report, a mural, or a presentation. What is being evaluated is the end product, not the process. Feedback was provided during instruction on the process, but now the final product will be evaluated.

Table 4.1. Short Constructed Response Rubric

Advanced	Proficient	Progressing	Beginning
All of the requirements for proficiency met, *plus*: The topic sentence utilizes unique language that entices the reader.	Creates a unique topic sentence that is clear and targeted.	The topic sentence is formulaic and may not be clearly expressed.	The topic sentence is not effective and misses the main point of the topic.

Table 4.2.   Extended Constructed Response Rubric

Advanced	Proficient	Progressing	Beginning
All of the requirements for proficiency met, *plus*: The writer may experiment with words and/or use figurative language and/or imagery.	Supporting details are relevant and provide important information about the topic. The writing has balance; the main idea stands out from the details. The writer seems in control and develops the topic in a logical, organized way.	The writer attempts to develop the topic in an organized way, but may falter in either logic or organization. The writer connects ideas with the specified topic implicitly rather than explicitly.	The writer has defined but not thoroughly developed the topic, idea, or story line; response may be unclear or sketchy or may read like a collection of thoughts from which no central idea emerges. Supporting details are minimal or irrelevant or no distinction is made between main ideas and details.

Every element applicable to the product should have an explanation to help the student understand why that level was chosen. The student can then use this information on their next presentation or product and improve as the year progresses.

Rubrics are generally classified into two types: analytic or holistic. The difference lies in whether the rubric is looking at one characteristic of the assignment at a time or treating the characteristics together. Analytic rubrics are those that treat the criterion separately, and holistic rubrics apply the criteria to provide an overall look at the work. The constructed response rubrics shared earlier were holistic. For the purposes of providing feedback to learners, analytic rubrics work best. They allow a more specific and targeted feedback to help the student make positive changes in the work. Holistic rubrics would be fine for a summative assessment where there will not be a chance to provide feedback for learning. If it is used to simply determine a final grade, a holistic rubric will make the process go faster because there is no need to mark specific criteria.

When creating a rubric, it is best to be general rather than task specific (Brookhart, 2013). Task-specific rubrics are limited and can only be used with the one task. A task-specific rubric may contain the solution to a problem; a general rubric will not. General rubrics have more application. They can be used to help students plan their work if shared at the beginning of the project. Students are able to develop independence and evaluate their work as they progress on the assignment. They also enable the teacher to focus on the skills required rather than the completion of the task. If the general rubric is well constructed, it will not need to be rewritten for each subsequent assignment.

When beginning the development of a new rubric, I have found that it is best to begin with the proficient level. What is it students need to be able to do to be considered proficient? Once that is written, it is easier to determine what would make a piece rise to the advanced level. What would be a bit over the expectations? It is also easier to write the lower levels because they are based upon the proficient level. What describes the level right below proficiency? Having the proficient language clearly written will help craft the language in the other areas. The description is what is important. That is what the students will use to evaluate their work, and you need to be clear about what is expected of them in the final work. It also must be clearly tied to the objectives included in the lesson.

While the rubric in table 4.3 has some description, it is not clear. I find myself wondering what exactly is "extraordinary style and voice." What might be "interesting voice"? Those are subjective terms. While you will not eliminate all subjectivity from a rubric, your goal should be to make it as clear as possible so that students know what they must do to be successful. You also want to be able to provide feedback, and the rubric should help you do that. Now let's look at this rubric with a few changes (table 4.4).

Table 4.3.   Informal Essay Rubric

	4. Advanced	3. Proficient	2. Developing	1. Emerging
Content/ Organization	Piece was written with extraordinary style and voice. Very informative and well organized.	Piece was written with interesting style and voice. Somewhat informative and well organized.	Piece was written with little style and voice. Gives some information but poorly organized.	Piece has no style or voice. Poorly written and contains no new information.
Mechanics	Virtually no spelling, grammar, or punctuation errors.	A few spelling, grammar, or punctuation errors.	A number of spelling, grammar, or punctuation errors.	So many spelling, grammar, or punctuation errors that it makes it difficult to understand.

Table 4.4.   Revised Informal Rubric

	4. Advanced	3. Proficient	2. Developing	1. Emerging
Content/ Organization	The author uses vivid words and phrases. The choice and placement of words seem natural, and not forced. The purpose of the writing is very clear, and there is strong evidence of attention to audience. There is one clear, well-focused topic. Main ideas are clear and are well supported by detailed and accurate information.	The author uses vivid words and phrases. The choice and placement of words is inaccurate at times and/or seems overdone. The purpose of the writing is somewhat clear, and there is some evidence of attention to audience. There is one clear, well-focused topic. Main ideas are clear but are not well supported by detailed information.	The author uses words that communicate clearly, but the writing lacks variety. The purpose of the writing is somewhat clear, but there is limited evidence of attention to audience. There is one topic. Main ideas are somewhat clear.	The writer uses a limited vocabulary. The purpose of the writing is unclear. The topic and main ideas are not clear.
Mechanics	All sentences are well constructed and have varied structure and length. The author makes no errors in grammar, mechanics, and/or spelling.	Most sentences are well constructed and have varied structure and length. The author makes a few errors in grammar, mechanics, and/or spelling, but they do not interfere with understanding.	Most sentences are well constructed, but lack variety of structure or length. The author makes several errors in grammar, mechanics, and/or spelling that interfere with understanding.	Sentences sound awkward, are repetitive, or are difficult to understand. The author makes numerous errors in grammar, mechanics, and/or spelling that interfere with understanding.

Before you continue to read, take a moment to reflect on the two rubrics shared. What are the main differences between the rubrics? How might the changes help you provide targeted feedback to the learner?

The second rubric explains in more detail what is expected of the learner. For an advanced student, I will look for vivid language. That is a term I would use during instruction. I would have provided lessons on using vivid language. They would also know what I mean by the term *varied sentences*, which is more meaningful than saying it was well organized. I have moved the sentence writing characteristics to mechanics because I think that is part of writing effective sentences, and I see that as more of a mechanics issue. I have provided the idea about having a main idea and support for it under organization because that is how I want students to organize their writing. I want them to have a clear purpose and focus while providing relevant support. This rubric clearly can be used by students to help plan and evaluate their own work.

In this chapter, we have looked at a variety of test items that can be used to assess the learning of students. It is important when designing an assessment that you choose the items that best match your objective. If the objective is to provide feedback and analyze the thinking of students, you make a different choice than if it is to make sure they have committed certain facts to memory. In the next chapter, we will put that to work and create some assessment questions around content.

Try It: Work with at least two others and choose a set of standards that you will be working with in the near future. As a team, create a few selected response questions, a short response, and an extended response. Create a holistic rubric for the short answer and an analytic rubric for the extended response. Split the work up to divide and conquer the task. Have a final discussion and evaluate the items. This task will simulate working with a grade-level team. This work is not done in isolation; teachers in most schools work collaboratively on assessment writing.

Chapter Five

Creating Formative Assessments

The reason for assessing in a classroom is to make inferences about the learning aimed at improving student outcomes. According to Ainsworth and Viegut (2006), when assessment is used diagnostically it is regarded as formative. Our point is to be able to use the results to diagnose next steps with our students and clarify the learning in the classroom. If the assessment is closely tied to the standard, it will allow better inferences to be made about the learner's understanding, which will result in a more effective acceleration or remediation plan. The assessments teachers create for the classroom will help clarify the curriculum, determine student readiness or understanding, and determine the effectiveness of the instruction (Popham, 2003).

Now it is time to write some assessment items. Remember that you will not be assessing every standard. Your team or school should have done some work and determined the most essential standards, as we discussed in chapter 2. That is a critical step in order to focus the efforts in the classroom. Those essential standards will be the ones that are assessed and monitored throughout the learning process. They are the ones that feedback will be given on to move the learning forward. The assessment has to be written so that it will provide the opportunity for feedback to improve learning. Remember, *it is not simply for a grade in a grade book.*

Once the standards are decided upon, it is time to begin to craft the assessment. As you recall from chapters 3 and 4, the questions should clearly match the standard. In order to do this, time must be taken to "unwrap the standard" (Ainsworth, 2003, p. 1) and determine what it is exactly the students must know and be able to do. In this step, we are clarifying the curriculum. It will help the teaching team determine what to teach and how to teach it. This process includes thinking about activities and experiences that must be included to provide students multiple opportunities to master the content. It will help make pedagogy choices as well as content choices. Some strategies will work better to meet the declared aims. It might necessitate that the teacher utilize cooperative grouping, or a Think-Pair-Share structure (Kagan, 1994). If part of the standard is that students need to be able to explain, the assessment instrument must give them opportunities to do that in a variety of ways. They have to be able to do that orally in peer groups and in writing. In both of those cases, they have to be provided specific and timely feedback in order to improve. Finally, our assessments will help us know how effective our instruction was with a particular group of learners. During the analysis, it might be beneficial to disaggregate the data so this can be further analyzed. Did the lesson work well for students? Which group demonstrated a clear increase in their understanding? The results will be used to evaluate the lesson and perhaps the pedagogy. It will be important to determine if the pedagogy was right for all learners. That might play a role in the reteaching. If one approach did not work, try another. It is important for the assessment to be written in a way that will enable us to make those kinds of inferences as well.

We will put Ainsworth's (2003) suggestion to work by first looking at the nouns and the verbs contained in the standard and matching them to Bloom's Taxonomy. The nouns in the standards will tell us what to teach (content) and the verbs will give us a clue as to the skills required by the students. The learning has to enable them to practice the skills and get meaningful feedback as we progress in the learning. Figure 5.1, provided by Transformative Inquiry Design for Effective Schools and Systems (http://www.tideseducation.org/), will help match the verbs to the correct level of Bloom's Taxonomy.

You see both the old and the new versions in the table. The new version uses verbs to describe the levels. That is important because it directly relates to what the students will be doing. We want the students to be active in their learning, which requires us to write items that allow that active participation. It acknowledges the iterative nature of learning and the fact that it is a learner-mediated process (Sousa & Tomlinson, 2011).

Below you will see three math content standards taken from the Indiana Department of Education website. This is from the document created in lieu of Common Core Standards. Again, it does not matter which standards you

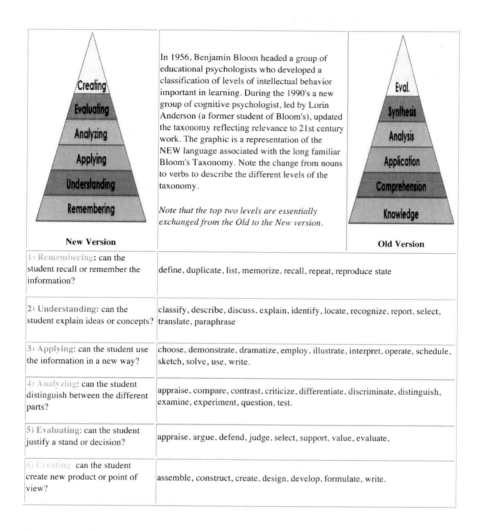

In 1956, Benjamin Bloom headed a group of educational psychologists who developed a classification of levels of intellectual behavior important in learning. During the 1990's a new group of cognitive psychologist, led by Lorin Anderson (a former student of Bloom's), updated the taxonomy reflecting relevance to 21st century work. The graphic is a representation of the NEW language associated with the long familiar Bloom's Taxonomy. Note the change from nouns to verbs to describe the different levels of the taxonomy.

Note that the top two levels are essentially exchanged from the Old to the New version.

New Version		Old Version
1) Remembering: can the student recall or remember the information?	define, duplicate, list, memorize, recall, repeat, reproduce state	
2) Understanding: can the student explain ideas or concepts?	classify, describe, discuss, explain, identify, locate, recognize, report, select, translate, paraphrase	
3) Applying: can the student use the information in a new way?	choose, demonstrate, dramatize, employ, illustrate, interpret, operate, schedule, sketch, solve, use, write.	
4) Analyzing: can the student distinguish between the different parts?	appraise, compare, contrast, criticize, differentiate, discriminate, distinguish, examine, experiment, question, test.	
5) Evaluating: can the student justify a stand or decision?	appraise, argue, defend, judge, select, support, value, evaluate,	
6) Creating: can the student create new product or point of view?	assemble, construct, create, design, develop, formulate, write.	

Figure 5.1.   Bloom's Taxonomy, Original and Revised.

are using; they are simply describing your learning outcomes. I have included a computation standard and two data analysis standards. You will also notice the processing standard.

    4.C.2: Multiply a whole number of up to four digits by a one-digit whole number and multiply two two-digit numbers, using strategies based on place value and the properties of operations. Describe the strategy and explain the reasoning.

4.DA.1: Formulate questions that can be addressed with data. Use observations, surveys, and experiments to collect, represent, and interpret the data using tables (including frequency tables), line plots, and bar graphs.

DA.3: Interpret data displayed in a circle graph.

PS.6: Attend to precision. Mathematically proficient students communicate precisely to others. They use clear definitions, including correct mathematical language, in discussion with others and in their own reasoning. They state the meaning of the symbols they choose, including using the equal sign consistently and appropriately. They express solutions clearly and logically by using the appropriate mathematical terms and notation. They specify units of measure and label axes to clarify the correspondence with quantities in a problem. They calculate accurately and efficiently and check the validity of their results in the context of the problem. They express numerical answers with a degree of precision appropriate for the problem context.

Let's look at the first standard listed. The first step is determining the nouns and the verbs contained in the standard (Ainsworth, 2003). You see them listed in figure 5.2. I try to list them directly across from one another so that I can match the content with the action. For instance, the first noun is *number*, and the students are expected to multiply them. After all of the nouns and verbs are listed, it is time to think about what exactly the students are required to do. This is where the verbs will be matched to the correct level in Bloom's Taxonomy. This is not an exact science; there may be some disagreement about the level, but that is when teachers can come together for discussion about what they should be expecting of students. Those can be rich discussions and result in a shared understanding of the work. It is important to have them in your grade-level meetings.

The questions I create for this standard must enable the students to apply reasoning skills when solving the problem. Simply giving them a problem and then providing a selection of answers will not be the best approach for this standard. I would not be able to fully analyze their gaps in understanding from a selected response item. For this particular standard, I would choose a short response format.

Sample Test Item: Solve the problem below using what you know about place value or the order of operations. Explain how you know your answer is reasonable, and briefly describe the steps you used to solve the problem.

Answer: 15×13

4.C.2: Multiply a whole number of up to four digits by a one-digit whole number and multiply two two-digit numbers, using strategies based on place value and the properties of operations. Describe the strategy and explain the reasoning.	
Nouns	*Verbs*
(whole) number *digit (one, two, four)* *value* *properties* *operation* *strategy* *reasoning* • *I have included some descriptors that will be of importance when creating the problems. I will need to have problems with varied numbers of digits because that it what the standard demands. I need to limit it to whole numbers as well.*	*multiply* *using* *describe* *explain* • *If I look back at Bloom's Taxonomy, I see that describe and explain are at the understanding level. However, students in this case need to explain their reasoning not their process. That element makes this standard more closely aligned to Level 4-Analysis.*

Figure 5.2. Unpacking Graphic Organizer.

Students could use a couple of approaches here, but I would be looking for them to use the numbers in a way that demonstrates the understanding of place value. For instance, they may multiply the 15 by 10 and then by 3 and add the products together, which demonstrates that they know the number 13 is made up of one 10 and a 3. This indicates an understanding of place value. Their written explanations about why they think their answer is reasonable will also give me information about their understanding. This write-up would only need to be a few sentences.

If you notice, the test item is directly using the verbs from the standard. I have asked them to *describe* how they solved the problem. They also have to *evaluate* the answer for reasonableness. This problem will also allow me to see if the process I taught is making sense to the students. If it is not, I may need a new approach. This assessment format can be repeated multiple times throughout the unit. The same directions can be used with another problem. The next time it might have a three-digit number and progress up to the required four digits. I may also differentiate the assessment by providing more difficult problems to those who are ready and remain at two digits for those who are struggling.

This item also can be used to provide feedback on the processing standard PS 6: Attend to precision. This one problem is providing the opportunity to give specific, targeted feedback to students and evaluate multiple standards at the same time. An important part of feedback is that it is clear and goal referenced (Wiggins, 2012). The standard is the goal, and the feedback should help students reach that goal. There is a lot of learning opportunity in this one question. Top it off with the fact that you only have to correct one problem, not a page of problems. It is a win for both teacher and student.

I would also have to develop a rubric for this question (see figure 5.3). I would include language about the solution being related to place value and also the process of analyzing the answer. I would borrow language from the process standard for this because it describes what the students should be able to do. I have made this as general as possible so I could use it for a variety of problems. It is not task specific. It is written in such a way that I am able to provide feedback on specific components. That will help to achieve the kind of feedback suggested by Wiggins (2012). I will also be able to group students based on the results. Some students may need to focus on the computation and others the ability to express the solution.

As far as pedagogy choices go for these two standards, I would want to include some direct teaching of the process of using place value in this way. I

Math Solution	Advanced	Proficient	Progressing	Beginning
Solution	The student has a correct solution.	The student has a correct solution.	The solution may not be correct.	The solution is not correct.
Process	The student may demonstrate more than one process.	The process is correct and clearly demonstrated with no computation errors.	The process is correct, but there may be minor computation errors.	The process in incorrectly applied and there are several errors in computation.
Expression	The student uses a variety of methods to demonstrate their thinking. They may include a model of the steps to their solution with each step explained.	They use clear definitions, including correct mathematical language, when explaining the solution and their reasoning. They express solutions clearly and logically by using the appropriate mathematical terms and notation.	They use vague definitions, but include some correct mathematical language when explaining the solution and their reasoning. They attempt to express solutions but it is difficult to follow the thinking.	They use vague definitions, and do not correctly use mathematical language when explaining the solution. The explanation is not developed in a way that enables the evaluator to understand their thinking.

Figure 5.3.   Math Solution Rubric.

would also want to provide students an opportunity to practice this process. I might use partner talk and problem solving, which would enable students to be supported at first in the process. I would also listen in on the talk occurring, which would give me an opportunity for immediate feedback or questions that will promote the development of understanding. I could also include the opportunity for partners to work with other groups to explain their thinking and ask questions. If I limited myself to direct instruction and individual practice, I would not be able to interact with individual students as much. The students would also not have the opportunity to practice their explaining in order to become more effective at demonstrating understanding. They will be required to explain their thinking on the assessment, so that must be part of the practice. If they simply solve problems, they will not be reaching the level of rigor in the standard.

Yorke (2003) describes formative assessment as "fundamentally a collaborative act," and it requires thoughtful interaction between teachers and students. It is in that interaction that learning is being refined. To borrow an idea from the leadership work of James Spillane (2006), leadership practice is generated in the interactions of leaders and followers. In this case, it is the leadership for learning in the classroom. The interaction will define the learning. It is an opportunity to clarify and refine the thinking about content. Do not miss the opportunity to have those interactions with students. If you tried to meet individually with every student to have those interactions, you would never make it around the classroom in a math block. By grouping students strategically, you can get to all students in the time period. It is the structure of the learning environment that will enable the interactions.

As far as individual practice goes, I might send home one or two problems for homework. I would also use one problem as a formative assessment after a couple of days of instruction. That might be a closure for a lesson, but it will act as a formative assessment. I would only give one problem, and it would have to be done independently. The students would be asked to explain their thinking as well. That problem would allow me to provide written feedback and begin a record of the feedback and responses the students give over time. This will enable me to see and communicate the progress to students, colleagues, administrators, and parents. The reality is that all of these stakeholders are interested in the progress of the students in your class. This kind of practice will help you collect information for conferences, grade-level meetings, and evaluations.

While the standards earlier led to a constructed response, some standards are better served by writing a selected response. If recall of information or a simple interpreting of data is the goal, a selected response will enable me to determine if the student has the knowledge. Let's look at another standard from the original list.

> **DA.3:** Interpret data displayed in a circle graph. This standard can be tested in a selected response format. As long as I give the students a graph they have never seen before, I can test their ability to interpret the graph through selected response. I can use a variety of question stems for that assessment. It is important to take into account all of the requirements for the items as I create the items for my test. Look back in chapter 3 for the guidelines.

I have used the graph shown in figure 5.4 to create a few selected response questions as a model.

Multiple Choice

Here I am using a familiar term. This is a straightforward interpretation.

Which of the lunch items do most of the students prefer? (I have listed the choices alphabetically.)

Lunch Preferences

■ Pizza   ■ Hamburgers   ■ Mac & Cheese   ■ Tacos

Figure 5.4.   Pie Graph for Assessment.

1. Hamburgers
2. Mac & Cheese
3. Pizza
4. Tacos

Binary Choice

This is another opportunity for interpretation. I have included the term *majority* because I want students to be able to express mathematical knowledge in a variety of ways using appropriate vocabulary. Do they associate the word *majority* with the word *most*? I have also required that they combine two sections of the graph to make this determination.

The majority of the students in the class would be happy if the cafeteria was serving hamburgers and tacos. (T/F)

Matching

This is giving the students a chance to interpret the sizes of the pie pieces in the graph. They would have to analyze a bit here. The 50% is clear and the 25% is clear, but they will have to make some decisions about the others. The correct answer is Mac & Cheese 15 and Tacos 10. That is also the only way it comes up to a total of 100%. This can relate to the processing standard as well.

Match the category in column A to the correct percentage in column B.

Column A	Column B
1. Pizza	A. 10%
2. Hamburgers	B. 15%
3. Mac & Cheese	C. 20%
4. Tacos	D. 25%
	E. 50%

Fill in the Blank

I would include a variety of questions here. It would be important to have more frames than answers and also that they could use the same answer more than once. This will force them to carefully read the phrases.

Use the word bank to complete the statements. You may use a term more than once. (pizza / tacos / hamburgers / mac & cheese)

Half of the class chose _____ as their favorite lunch.

Try It 1: Create selected response questions related to the graph above. Share them with a partner or in a large group. Evaluate how well the question matches the criteria shared in chapter 3. Can you make them better? I have included the percentages in the graph in figure 5.5. How might you reframe the questions to include that information? (Example items at the end of the chapter.)

In this chapter, we have looked at the process of unpacking a standard and writing an assessment that will fit our purpose. The assessments will help make inferences about the learning. The better aligned the assessment is with

Pets

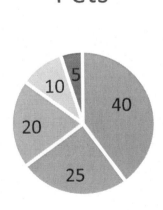

cats   dogs   hamsters   snakes   fish

Figure 5.5.   Pie Graph for Practice.

the standard, the better it will be to make those inferences. The formative assessments created for the classroom help clarify the curriculum, determine student readiness or understanding, and determine the effectiveness of the instruction (Popham, 2003).

It does not matter what subject matter you are working with; the process to write the assessment remains the same.

Determine the standards you will be focused upon for the unit. Your grade-level team or school might have developed power standards, which will help with the process. If not, you have to determine what the most important ones will be for you. Refer back to chapter 2 and make sure your standards are essential. You will not assess every single standard listed in your state standards document.

Break the standards apart by focusing on the nouns and verbs. This step will clarify what the students need to be able to do. It will also help you make pedagogy choices about how it will be best taught. The verbs will lead you to the level of rigor (Bloom's Taxonomy) that the standard must be assessed at in order to determine student understanding.

Write the assessment. This is where you will choose the best format for the assessment. The format is really determined by the level of rigor. If the assessment requires a recall of information or an identification, a selected response might work well. If the student is required to analyze, synthesize, or compare and contrast, then a constructed response might work better for your purposes.

Give the assessment and analyze the results. This is where you will determine if the students understand and if the pedagogy was successful. This analysis has its own structure, which will be covered in chapter 6. It is this process that will lead to your next steps with students.

Ideally, this process of writing assessments will be shared by a grade-level team. It would best serve the team for all to be giving the same assessment so that comparisons can be made. Everyone should be on the same page here. As you look at the results with the structure that will be provided for you in chapter 6, the team will be able to plan interventions. You may even be able to creatively group students across the grade level for intervention and acceleration based on the results. Those kinds of decisions should always be based upon data, and that brings us to our next chapter.

Try It 2: Use the standard below to practice the process of unpacking. You can use the organizer format shared earlier in the chapter, or another one that works for you. The point is to unpack it and then create some problems to go with the standard that can act as a formative assessment. I have provided a few guiding questions here for your consideration. What must be included in the problems you create? What would be considered proficient? What kind of assessment will give the students the opportunity to express the understanding at the correct level? What might their response look like? What pedagogy might you use? Write a test item and share it with another team for feedback. (See figure 5.6 at the end of the chapter for an example.)

4.DA.1: Formulate questions that can be addressed with data. Use observations, surveys, and experiments to collect, represent, and interpret the data using tables (including frequency tables), line plots, and bar graphs.

The following are selected response examples for Try It 1:

Multiple Choice

Which two choices when combined will represent 50% of the class?

  a. Cats and Dogs
  b. Dogs and Fish
  c. Cats and Hamsters
  d. Dogs and Snakes

Binary Choice

Cats and dogs are the two most popular pet choices in our class. Y/N

Matching

Match the percentage with the categories that equal that amount.

A. 30%	1. Cats and fish
B. 45%	2. Dogs and cats
C. 55%	3. Snakes, fish, and hamsters
D. 65%	4. Cats, dogs, and fish
E. 70%	5. Dogs and fish
	6. Dogs, hamsters, and snakes

Fill in the Blank

Use the word bank to complete the statements. You may use a term more than once. (pizza / tacos / hamburgers / mac & cheese)

One quarter of the class chose _____ as their favorite lunch.

Figure 5.6 shows the possible response examples for Try It 2. As you can see, it is not going to be an assessment where students can simply answer some questions about a graph. The interpreting in this case should be tied with the formulation of questions because that is the ultimate goal here. It extends the work of DA.3 to another level. Therefore, when planning I would begin with DA.3 and build from there. It would allow for scaffolding of the process. I might also include some sentence frames as a beginning point for students when they are constructing their questions, which would be especially necessary for English learners. Including the answering of the questions they create to demonstrate that they are interpreting the graph correctly would also

4.DA.1: Formulate questions that can be addressed with data. Use observations, surveys, and experiments to collect, represent, and interpret the data using tables (including frequency tables), line plots, and bar graphs.	
Nouns	Verbs
Questions Data Observations Surveys Experiments Tables (frequency tables) Line plots Bar graphs • I am going to have to plan several opportunities for students to collect data and create graphs from that data. I will also need to guide them in the creating of questions about the data in the tables. That is much different than simply answering questions.	Formulate Collect (needs to be done and assessed in class-while active in the process) Represent interpret • Students must be involved in the collecting of the data as well as being able to represent it in a variety of ways. They also have to be able to interpret the results of observations experiments, surveys, and graphs. They have to be able to formulate questions about the data represented not simply answer questions. While DA3 asks them only to interpret, this one is asking them to do more with the data. They have to use it to create (represent) something. That is the highest level of Bloom's Taxonomy. (Level 6- Creating)

Figure 5.6. Example Solution.

be a consideration for my assessment. In this case, we would need a multi-step process and a rubric that included both the interpretation and the creation of questions about the graph. That process can include representing, interpreting, and formulating by simply giving the students raw data and having them create the graph and questions, which would enable me to see if they were having trouble with any of those elements. It also would include the process skill. All of this will have to be on the rubric so that feedback can be given to the student. It would require us changing the previous rubric slightly. The expression part would have to reflect the creation of the graph, the questions, and the interpretation of the graph.

Chapter Six

Data-Driven Decision Making

The Learning Loop

In the previous chapter, we looked at the creation of assessment items that are aligned to the standards. This chapter will outline for you what to do with the results of those assessments. The assessments must be analyzed in a manner that allows for the identification of gaps for remediation or the need for acceleration. That is what the TIDES Learning Loop is aimed at (see figure 6.1). This process will help fine-tune instruction and monitor student progress toward goals. Ideally, it should be adopted on a whole school level, but if it is not adopted by the whole school, a grade level can be doing work with this cycle in mind.

STEP 1

In the previous chapters, we unpacked standards and designed some common assessments that are ideal for using in the TIDES Learning Loop (Ainsworth, 2003). In the first step of the cycle, teachers have created a plan of instruction and an assessment to measure that instruction. This would be the assessment that has been created with the unpacked standards discussed in previous chapters. This work is best done in a collaborative format so that all are in agreement that the created assessments are measuring what they claim to be measuring. At an agreed upon time, the assessment is given and scored by each individual teacher. After each teacher has done this independently, the team can compile and present the whole grade-level information in some

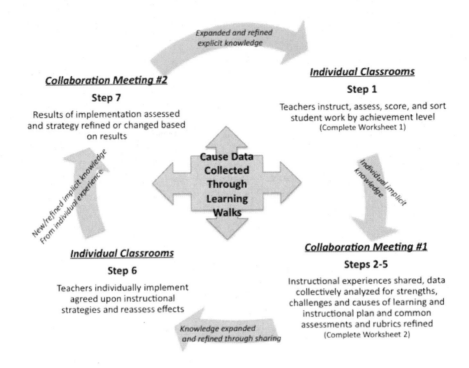

Figure 6.1. TIDES Learning Loop for Instructional Improvement. Courtesy Transformative Inquiry Design for Effective Schools and Systems (TIDES).

format. Technology could be used to make this process streamlined. It is dependent upon what you have available at your school. A table of some sort where the student names can be compiled so it is easy to see where they fall in relation to proficiency is helpful. Table 6.1 is one example of such a table. This will help to plan groups for remediation, continued support, or acceleration. This collective process is actually quite fast if everyone has done the scoring.

As you can see, the teacher's names are on the far left of the table. Each teacher has broken down their class by the results of the assessment, which would be read going across the table. Going down in each ranking, advanced to below basic and far below basic, you can see the students from the grade level who fall into these categories. The charting allows the team to consider several possibilities for grouping the students. There might be a time where the students are grouped together for specific interventions and do not stay in their home classrooms. It is also possible that each teacher might take care of the interventions in their own classrooms. The interventions have to specifi-

Table 6.1.   Grade Level Results Table

	Advanced (4)	Proficient (3)	Basic (2)	Below Basic (1) & Far Below Basic (0)
Smith	#4: 13% Student names: Johnny, Marco, Sally, Jane	#12: 40% Student names: Bill, Lori, Cathy, Joe, Ned, Maria, Francis, Bart, Terri, Yvonne, Sharon, Carl	#9: 30% Student names: Dave, Laura, Tiffany, Doug, Dylan, Tammy, Karen, Linda, Mary	#5: 17% Student names: Kelly, Olivia, Joey, Tom, Danny
Miller	#4: 13% Student names: Josephine, Martin, Sammy, JoAnn	#11: 37% Student names: Robert, Carol, Chris, Joseph, Nancy, Matt, Frank, Kevin, Erin, Carolyn, Peggy	#12: 40% Student names: Nicole, Mike, Steven, Christopher, Joan, Tracey, Janet, Vanessa, Jessie, Paul, Veronica, William	#3: 10% Student names: Beatrice, Alice, Kandace
Johnson	#2: 7% Student names: Donna, Marti	#9: 30% Student names: Catherine, Hilda, Austin, Leslee, Victoria, Pat, Dean, Jack, Nathalie	#15: 50% Student names: Jim, Michael, Jerry, Giovanna, Susan, Sandy, Ellen, Kayla, Peter, Doris, Hugh, Thomas, Justin, Billy, George	#4: 13% Student names: Elaine, Christine, Eileen, Mark

cally address the needs of the groups. Chapter 7 will cover the differentiation for specific target groups in more depth.

In order to make the placements, the team must decide on what would be included in the evaluation of the students. It could be based solely on the rubric scores assigned for the responses. However, there is some room for adjustments because student understanding is more complex than the results of one assessment. A teacher might shift a student's rating based on other information as well. The data sources are dependent upon the choice of the district or school. Some data, like that generated from the holistic and analytic grading, might be compiled by the teachers. Other data might be supplied by programs such as Measures of Academic Progress (MAPS), an adaptive testing program developed by Northwest Evaluation Association. These kinds of programs provide a plethora of information that can be used in a variety of ways. Each program has its benefits and drawbacks. I think the assessment tool should be evaluated by the team as to the accuracy of the information. That is why it is important for you to understand assessment and question creation. Your decisions need to be made on the best available information regarding student cognition.

STEP 2

Looking at Student Work

The discussion at the collaboration meeting will focus upon the gaps in understanding. Each group of learners must be talked about by examining the work. In the late 1990s, Annenberg introduced educators to protocols for looking at student work. Schools that engage in this process see a significant change in student performance (Datnow, Park, & Wohlstetter, 2007; Dial, 2011). However, one notable shift in the TIDES protocol, shared in figure 6.1, is the focus on teachers' instructional practices. The earlier protocols identified differences in student performance, but there was little focus on what teachers did in the classroom and how they might change their instructional practices to improve student learning. This process will help drive changes in the classroom that will result in deeper learning for the students.

Each teacher should bring examples of the advanced, proficient, basic, and below basic to serve as evidence of the level of learning. This will ensure that the team is thinking about proficiency in the same way. Looking at the student work, and having conversations about why and how it clearly demonstrates an assigned level, will help the team members reach a shared understanding of the work. The team must be in agreement about what work at each of the levels looks like. If one teacher is not holding their students to the same standard for proficiency, the data will be skewed. It also will be giving students a false sense of accomplishment and interfere with providing meaningful feedback for learning. This process of looking at student work is a powerful practice. It moves beyond the assignment of the grade and allows the deeper review of learning. The focus questions in table 6.2 are some that can frame this discussion. When examining the work for strengths, there must be clear evidence of understanding. Through this process, the evidence of what students know and gaps in understanding should be clearly articulated. Those gaps might be in understanding process or content as discussed previously.

Concentrating on the strengths and weaknesses will enable the prioritizing of the needs. Teachers cannot address every gap in a two-week intervention, but they can target specific needs that will move the work and student thinking forward. The analysis should end up identifying one or two needs that can be addressed in the next steps.

Drawing Meaningful Conclusions

It is important to make inferences about the learning. The inferences made must move into the why. They should be focused on the cognition. What is happening or not happening in the thought process of the student? The ability to make solid inferences about the work is dependent on the assessment being written in such a way that allows that analysis. It is why writing the assessment so that those gaps can be analyzed is so important. If the items were written in a way that did not allow students to completely express their understanding, we will not be able to determine the next steps to take.

One trap that many fall into is making inferences that are about effort rather than understanding. "Joey just never tries." That type of inference will not help you identify a gap. Stay away from the blame game. If Joey is really that disconnected, find a way to connect him in the learning. That is another issue. The point of the inference is to make a plan for the intervention. "I wonder if Joey is having difficulty because he does not have control of _____, and that is interfering with his ability to do _____." Meaningful inferences result in an idea for action, which are the next steps in the chart. If I can identify what might be interfering with success, I can plan an intervention to deal with the issue and plan an effective intervention.

As you can see, this concentrates on the proficient-level students. The students here have control of the content. However, they might need to be supported with more practice or practice that allows a deepening of the content at the standard for the grade level. The work students will be engaged in doing might be guided by the teacher, but, most likely, it will be independent work. They have the precursor skills necessary to continue the learning. They might need some support, but it will not be as comprehensive as a student who is working below grade level.

Table 6.2. Sample Analysis Chart

Levels	Strengths: What can the students do well? What do they control? What content do they control/understand?	Weaknesses: Where are they going wrong? What is the misunderstanding? What is interfering with the success? What are the gaps in knowledge or skill? What is the prioritized need? What will make the most difference?	Next Steps/ Strategy: What will you do to address the weaknesses? How often will you do it? How will you measure the effectiveness?
Proficient	Students can solve with using arrays, drawings and quantities (step 2).	Students are confused by the unknown. This confusion is leading to the lack of clarity in explanation and the incorrect solution (step 2, inference).	Provide students with a structure for solving the unknown. Model the use in small groups and then have them work independently on finding solutions (step 3). At the end of week 1, reassess to see if they are mastering the idea. If they begin to show an understanding, move to unequal groups within 100 (step 4).

You can see that the inference about the students' work is that they may have some confusion about the unknown quantity. They may be all right if the numbers are supplied in a problem, but they may not be able to figure it out if there is an unknown quantity. In order to help predict students' limits, questions in the pre-assessment would have been crafted to assess their ability to work with known and unknown numbers. That would help me, as the teacher, to determine where the students' understanding might be limited. I would use their understanding of one to build understanding of the other. As you can see in table 6.2, I have also determined the next steps that should be taken with students in the proficient range. (The standard is to use multiplication and division within 100 to solve word problems in situations involving equal groups, arrays, and measurement quantities, e.g., by using drawings and equations with a symbol for the unknown number to represent the problem.) Refer to the appendix at the end of this chapter for the complete chart. Since I think they need a structure, I need to find one to support their understanding. I have also thought about when I will monitor the learning. How will I specifically do that? What strategy would be best to use to teach and practice the skill? That brings us to step 3 in the TIDES process, which is designing the intervention.

STEP 3

Teachers cooperatively design the intervention in this step of the process. They will determine what will be done for each group and what instructional structure will be used. Here the team will decide upon common strategies. How the information will be delivered is as important as what will be delivered. As you can see in table 6.2, the next step is to provide a structure, which could be a graphic organizer, to aid the students in solving for the unknown. It is important for the next step to include some description of the pedagogy. It will be important that all proficient students across the grade level are getting the same level of support and instruction. Both Hattie (1992) and Marzano (2003) have contributed to understanding of the effect size of certain strategies. "The effect size reports how many standard deviations the average score in the experimental group (the group that uses the instructional strategy) is above the average score in the control group (the group that did not use the instructional strategy)" (Marzano, 2003). Since we are not doing research, we want all of the students to benefit from the planned intervention so all must receive it.

Marzano has also provided a list of nine essential and effective instructional strategies. The strategies can be used in all content areas. They are proven strategies that result in higher levels of student learning. This list can be drawn from in step 3 when the team is designing interventions. The nine strategies include identifying similarities and differences, summarizing and note taking, reinforcing effort, homework and practice, nonlinguistic representation, cooperative learning, setting goals and providing feedback, generating and testing hypotheses, and using cues, questions, and advanced organizers (2003).

The first of the nine is identifying similarities and differences. By incorporating comparing and contrasting, students can understand complex problems by breaking them into simpler components. As a part of this strategy, a teacher might use a Venn diagram or T-charts to compare, contrast, and classify items. Students might be encouraged to create metaphors or analogies as a demonstration of this kind of thinking (Marzano, 2003). Students could use visual images as well to compare and contrast ideas. The possibilities are endless, really. The important point is that they are supported in clarifying their understanding by using this kind of thinking. They might be able to use a T-chart that allows them to see the differences between solving for the known and the unknown.

Another of Marzano's (2003) nine is the use of summarizing and note taking. It is important to take a broad look at summarizing. It is not limited to writing a summary. Students can be engaged in verbal summary, which would be an important consideration for students who struggle with writing. This would include English learners as well as students with an identified learning disability. Note taking could be done with a structure that would enable students to revise and add to their notes as their understanding deepens. The process of note taking enables students to determine the most important elements. It provides a structure for students to eliminate distracting details, which often confuse them. In the math example, the learning experience could contain opportunities for the students to take notes on the process they are learning.

Reinforcing the effort of students and finding a way to provide recognition is another of the essential strategies. This enables the students to see the connection between effort and results. Any progress toward the learning goal should be recognized. This feedback will help the students stay focused and motivated as they continue to improve. This can be done verbally or in writing. This strategy is one that will enable the teacher and student to develop that trusting relationship that helps students see their potential rather than their limitations. This can be implemented easily in our example. Students might become frustrated in the process, but they can be verbally praised for their efforts, which will help them persevere.

Homework should have a prescribed purpose and enable the student to practice the important concepts they have learned (Marzano, 2003). I always think of homework as practice when the coach is not there. Athletes practice shooting hoops or hitting baseballs outside of a guided practice. Academics is the same. Students need to practice the skills and the thinking in order to develop the ability to use the skills well. It should be something that can be done independently and may have to be differentiated for the variety of learners in the classroom. They should not be overwhelmed. A student does not have to be required to solve 50 problems; they can do just a few for practice at home. They can come in with their questions the next day. That is more likely to move the learning forward. It is also more likely to be completed. This is especially true of students who struggle. The requirements for homework can be different for the different levels. More on that idea will be discussed in chapter 7.

Nonlinguistic representation stimulates brain activity. Pictures and simple phrases can be used to help a student express or understand relationships in the content. Again, it allows for a more divergent thinking to happen. The representation can be given to, or created by, the student. That decision would be determined by the context. This can also be used as a strategy within another of Marzano's (2003) nine, cooperative learning. As a part of the cooperative learning task, the group might be tasked with creating a visual representation of vocabulary or content. That way, they are also engaging in discussions and have both individual and group accountability. There are a variety of cooperative group structures that are effective. It would depend on the task. Groups, in my experience, should be kept to no more than four. That way all can be involved. If the number gets too high, there tends to be more off-task behavior. The math example could lend itself to working in partners or groups. They may be tasked with developing a poster to help them remember the steps in the process.

Setting goals and providing feedback is why you look at the data in the first place. Positive feedback is important. Tell the students what they are doing well. Some feedback should be corrective in nature and help the students see the next steps they must take to improve. It is helpful to use a rubric for this. The language is present in the rubric, and the teacher can provide a specific example of how the students might change something to move to the next level using the rubric language. Having students give one another feedback is good as well. There should be some structure for this. I have found that when students are able to do this, they become more effective at looking at their own work as well.

The last two strategies relate to helping the students think. When students generate and test a hypothesis, they are using both inductive and deductive reasoning. The cues, questions, and organizers provided to students can also aid them in this kind of thinking. By asking both open and closed questions, teachers can help students make deductions and clarify connections.

By choosing an effective strategy, the likelihood of success is raised. The strategy should match the goal. Use the one that best serves the needs of the students. All teachers should use the strategy as a part of the intervention designed. If one teacher fails to do that, it might interfere with the success of the intervention. The grade level is a team. Members have to be willing to do their part in the process with fidelity. When this is not adhered to, conflict arises. That interferes with everyone's success—especially the students'. One team member might need support implementing something, and the other members should be ready to give that support.

An important element of the plan is to determine the time and frequency of the intervention. This is especially important for the students in the below-level and far-below-level groups. These are the groups that will need more frequent meetings in order to move to the proficient level. In order for the intervention to have the desired effect, it must match the prioritized need. It should be focused on improving the learning gap identified in step 2. The differentiation described in previous tables would ideally take place during independent work time. The teacher would likely have time available during independent work time to spend time with selected students or groups. Time is the most precious commodity in a classroom. Time can be used to intervene with math in the morning or during a writing block. It does not only have to occur during math instruction. Teachers will need to be creative in finding time to meet with the groups they have identified. When doing an intervention, short times are best. The groups would only meet for 10 minutes at the most, but it would be a focused 10 minutes. In the completed chart shown in the appendix at the end of the chapter, you can see that not all of the groups would be meeting daily. The students with the most need get the teacher for more time through the week.

A second possible structure is a rotation of groups to teachers in the grade level. Perhaps three times a week a rotation could occur that would allow one teacher to work with a specific group. Depending upon the group assigned, the teacher will set up the learning environment to best suit the needs of the students. The important point is that every child should have either an enrichment of the skill or a further learning to help them master the goal. Many schools set aside time in the day for this kind of rotation. They use a variety of names for it, but it helps teachers get focused on success for all students.

STEP 4

The last step is creating a goal for the learning. It is the goal that will help determine if the intervention was successful. This is the place for a SMART goal (Doran, 1981). A SMART goal has the following criteria met: it is specific, measurable, attainable, realistic, and timely.

Specific: What exactly will be accomplished and how?

Measurable: What tools will be used to measure the attainment of the goal?

Attainable: The goal needs to be able to be attained with planned supports in the time given.

Realistic: Does it represent a logical growth?

Timely: Is there a time line suggested in the goal? (year, two weeks, a month)

Example

SMART goal: This year, 80% of all 3rd graders will demonstrate proficiency in reading comprehension as measured by the ISTEP and local measures assessments. This goal clearly defines what the expected results will be and when it should be achieved. It would be an end of the year goal. Interim goals would need to be developed as a part of the work toward the end of the year goal. It would be important to keep this in mind all year to make sure the team is working to accomplish the year-long goal.

For the example shared earlier:

SMART goal (based on the inference table 6.2): Students need to create an array or other visual in order to see the connection between the known and the unknown in division problems. As a result of the three-times-a-week intervention group *using nonlinguistic representation* when solving division problems, 22 of the 36 students in the basic column will move to proficiency as measured by the teacher-created assessment given at the end of week 2.

Notice that the strategy is mentioned in the goal. Teachers will have to agree to the strategy and all use it with their intervention groups. The above goal is specifically focused on one group. It states clearly how often the intervention will happen, what the teachers will do, what growth is desired, and how/when success will be measured.

Try It: Using table 6.1, create a SMART goal for the advanced, proficient, basic, and below basic students. You can begin by using the sentence frame provided:

As a result of _____, _____ students in the _____
group will _____ as measured by _____.

Share it in your group. Evaluate using the criteria below:

Specific: What exactly will be accomplished and how?

Measurable: What tools will be used to measure the attainment of the goal?

Attainable: The goal needs to be able to be attained with planned supports in the time given.

Realistic: Does it represent a logical growth?

Timely: Is there a time line suggested in the goal? (year, two weeks, a month)

"If you fail to plan, you are planning to fail!"—Benjamin Franklin

Let's go back to the quote from chapter 2. Planning is the most important part of teaching and learning. Without a clear plan, a teacher or a team will wander off the path and lose track of their ultimate goal. Coming back together every week to see the progress toward the goal is critical for long-term success.

This information is not theory; it is from personal experience. For several years, I was part of turnaround efforts in public schools. It became my work by accident. I did not set out to take a role in teacher leadership with that focus. However, when I was presented with the opportunity, it became my passion.

Just as there are times when sports teams come together and have success at a high level, there are times when that can happen with teacher teams in schools. Teacher teams can be a Super Bowl team! I was honored to lead such a team. I worked with two fabulous, committed teachers as part of a turnaround effort for a failing school. The school had made it to the five-year mark and was still failing. The scores had not improved enough after five years of being labeled as poor performing. This resulted in the complete restructuring of the school in order to change the culture, which meant the leadership changed and most of the teaching staff changed. My teammates, Rosario Murdoch and Stephanie Oliveri, were among the best instructors I have had the privilege of working with in my time in the classroom. Together we were unstoppable.

Our success came from focus and sharing data and strategies that worked for our students. We grouped our students in a fluid manner and met more than once a week to talk about progress and student need. We got our egos out of the way and concentrated on the needs of the students. I was committed to having the students with the highest needs in the lowest ratio classroom, which meant that Rosario and I would have to take on more students than we were contracted to have in our classrooms. No problem. It was the best for the students. Because our other classes were ready for the instruction and needed less intervention, we were able to serve more students. Was I popular with union representatives? No. Did I care? No. Was my team increasing student understanding and success? Yes. That is all we cared about.

As you can see from the data in table 6.3, we were successful with the students. This is a cohort comparison, so you must look at the year prior to see the growth for the cohort. Our work at the school started in 2007. You can see our first year the success of the cohort was raised by 40%. At the beginning of the 2008 school year, only 13% of our incoming students were testing proficient, but by the end 64% were in the proficient range. That success was followed up the next year as well with an increase from 30% to 74%. That change came from looking at student work and data and letting it tell us what to do for student success.

You can see that in our first year in math we did not make the necessary growth. The following year that changed. How? By creating a tighter focus on the link between assessment and teaching. We listened to the data and

Table 6.3. Standardized Test Scores

HARVEST (pseudonym) ALL STUDENTS: Language Arts

YEAR	2nd Grade	3rd Grade	4th Grade	5th Grade	6th Grade
2006	21%	20%	28%	19%	15%
2007	20%	13%	61%	19%	36%
2008	40%	30%	64%	52%	40%
2009	40%	31%	74%	70%	78%

HARVEST ALL STUDENTS

YEAR	2nd Grade	3rd Grade	4th Grade	5th Grade	6th Grade
2006	42%	53%	28%	26%	15%
2007	50%	35%	58%	26%	22%
2008	48%	71%	76%	61%	55%
2009	67%	79%	82%	85%	80%

made changes in our practice that helped all students succeed. We followed a similar process as the one shared in this chapter. The TIDES process is more refined and structured and even more powerful than what we had. This works, and it will work for you.

The appendix shows the complete analysis chart. The standard is to use multiplication and division within 100 to solve word problems in situations involving equal groups, arrays, and measurement quantities, for example, by using drawings and equations with a symbol for the unknown number to represent the problem.

In this chapter, we have looked at a process for remediation and acceleration. While it may seem time consuming, it will streamline with more experience. The first few times will be more time consuming, but then it will become how you think about students. When that paradigm shift happens, it will become second nature. Just like when you were learning to drive, it was totally consuming. You had to do everything methodically, but after a while, it became second nature and did not require as much effort. This will be the same, I promise. If you run into problems, contact me; I am always ready to help.

How to effectively differentiate will be covered in the next chapter. That is another element of a successful classroom. All students will be getting what they need rather than all students doing the same work. Students need to be met where they are rather than where we think they should be. They do not all walk in the classroom with the same readiness level. We need to be able to assess their needs and respond to ensure their success.

APPENDIX: COMPLETE ANALYSIS CHART

Levels: Above, Proficient, Basic, and Below Basic / Far Below Basic

Strengths: What can the students do well? What do they control? What content do they control/understand?

Weaknesses: Where are they going wrong? What is the misunderstanding? What is interfering with the success? What are the gaps in knowledge or skill? What is the prioritized need? What will make the most difference?

Next Steps/Strategy: What will you do to address the weaknesses? How often will you do it? How will you measure the effectiveness?

Level: Above

The students in this section probably have control of the content or the skill. They are, most likely, ready to move to the next level. How will you extend the learning? Will they work independently on a project or different level of problem? Might they work as partners? Will you engage them with questioning or have a product they will produce to demonstrate understanding?

Strengths: Can solve problems using all of the strategies with ease.

Weaknesses: Students need to be challenged to create and not only solve problems. They are ready for a more difficult application of the same strategies (unequal groups).

Next Steps / Strategy: Students need to be introduced to unequal groups. Should expose them to problems within 1000. They can also be stretched to create their own word problems.

Level: Proficient

The students here have control of the content, but might need to be supported with more practice or practice that allows a deepening of the content at the standard for the grade level. The work students will be engaged in doing might be guided by the teacher, but, most likely, it will be independent work.

Strengths: Students can solve with using arrays, drawings, and quantities.

Weaknesses: Students are confused by the unknown. This confusion is leading to the lack of clarity in explanation and the incorrect solution (inference).

Next Steps / Strategy: Provide students with a structure for solving the unknown. Model the use in small groups and then have them work independently on finding solutions. At the end of week 1, reassess to see if they are mastering the idea. If they begin to show an understanding, move to unequal groups within 100.

Level: Basic

The students here are almost to the proficient level. They may have some conceptual misunderstandings. It might necessitate taking part of the skill or concept and providing specific feedback and practice in order to move the work to the proficient level. This might be done in a small group. It might be that the teacher works with them a few times during the intervention period. They will need to have an assessment at the end of the intervention period to make sure that time resulted in more understanding. It is important to monitor the effectiveness of the intervention.

Strengths: Students are able to use the arrays. They struggle when there is no visual. Do not seem to understand the process for solving unknowns. Students have better control over multiplication rather than division.

Weaknesses: Students need to create an array or other visual in order to see the connection between the known and the unknown in division problems.

Next Steps / Strategy: Work in small groups three times a week to focus on tying the visual to the mathematical expression using division problems. Students will create the visuals rather than have them created for them. Assess after two weeks of intervention (only division).

Level: Below Basic / Far Below Basic

These are the students who are, most likely, missing some precursor knowledge. They will need the most intervention to make the progress that will be necessary to get to the proficient level. The choice for intervention efforts should be made with thought about what will move their understanding to the next level. Again, they will need an assessment geared to the work that was concentrated on for the intervention period. What is being done has to result in positive progress.

Strengths: Students are not able to answer any questions without error. They are not able to effectively use the pictures to solve problems.

Weaknesses: The numbers might be too large for them to easily comprehend. Moving to simpler numbers (within 50) might help with developing the ability to effectively use the strategies (inference).

Next Steps / Strategy: Work with the group daily for one week on using arrays only with multiplication. Use at least one formative assessment during the week to check progress. Work with groups daily for second week and apply the strategies to division problems. Assess at the end of week 2: two multiplication problems and two division problems.

Chapter Seven

Differentiation

Content, Process, and Product

Differentiation is something talked about with great fervor these days. However, it is not really new. Teachers have always known that students do not walk into their classrooms with the same skills and readiness for learning. Some of that is because brain development varies between children. A child's date of birth is not a clear indication of their readiness to learn or what supports they will need (Sousa & Tomlinson, 2011). Some variance is due to the gaps in their learning because of school attendance or quality. Not all students receive high quality instruction, which puts them at a disadvantage because they are not fully prepared to build new knowledge required in the current grade. Whatever the reason, teachers must effectively work with students in order to help them build their understanding. That work will look different depending on the readiness of the students. That is, at the core, what differentiation is about: providing what is needed.

It is important to remember that differentiation is not a list of what to do with each student. While there are effective strategies, like the ones shared in chapter 6, it is up to the teacher to determine what will work with the individuals in his or her class. The strategies listed by Marzano (2003) are likely to work with a broad range of learners, but these strategies may need to be tweaked to work with a specific group of learners. Those decisions are best made by classroom teachers.

Differentiation can be defined as the teacher's response to the learner's needs (Sousa & Tomlinson, 2011). That response is impacted by the perspective and the mind-set of the teacher. Ultimately, a teacher should be operating with a mind-set that has student success as the only acceptable learning outcome. Carol Dweck (2006) explains that the mind-sets teachers might approach this work with are either a "fixed" or a "growth" mind-set. A teacher with a fixed mind-set views a student as either capable or not in a specific domain. A teacher with this mind-set may feel that a student is genetically predisposed to be good at math, for example. This is probably why most teachers did not address my math needs in elementary school. Instead they, most likely, attributed it to the fact that I was not able in that content area. However, that was not true. I am capable, but I needed an approach that would enable me to learn. Many students are that way. Fixed mind-set teachers might claim that they taught the content, but the student did not learn it because of laziness, lack of ability, or some other factor not attributable to the teacher. They are not likely to think that the student did not learn because the input was not comprehensible for him. On the other hand, teachers with a growth mind-set do not deny the genetic component, but they perceive it as a starting point rather than a limitation. With focused attention and the right support, they have the belief that a student can succeed in any content area. Teachers with this mind-set are willing to examine the needs of the student and make changes in the instruction or content to ensure student learning. When students don't learn, the first response is to examine why that occurred and create a plan to deal with the obstacles. They recognize that the obstacle might be the pedagogy. They are willing to make changes if it means that students will understand content in a deeper manner as a result. Put yourself in the shoes of a doctor for a moment. If you try a treatment and it does not work for the patient, you would change the treatment plan. You would not blame the patient for not responding; you would seek out something that worked. The same is true for learning. Not all students will respond to the same pedagogy. Be willing to try something new.

It takes an examination of belief systems to know what mind-set teachers come to this work with, and it should be done because it impacts everything one does with a student. It will also determine the success with differentiation in the class. A teacher with a fixed mind-set is not likely to have as much success with differentiation in a classroom. Take a moment to honestly reflect on how you think about a lesson when the students did not learn. Where does your mind-set fall?

Students also come to their work with a mind-set. They may have heard messages about not being good in something, and they feel that they won't be successful. In many cases, that is the first step in successful differentiation in the classroom. Every student needs to see the connection between how they learn and success in learning. Effort certainly plays a role, but if they are doing the wrong work over and over, they will not want to put in the work. If they see success, effort will increase, and it will create a positive learning loop. There is a great energy that comes from success. That energy will help the student persevere through challenges that are bound to arise as they are learning (Dial, 2015). Through differentiation students will also develop the ability to guide their own learning and become independent of the teacher. Ultimately, that is what leads to being a lifelong learner. It is what we say we want for students. Lifelong learners are seekers of knowledge; they do not only learn when the teacher makes them do it.

In order to be able to differentiate, teachers need to have a clear focus for the learning. That is the work done in previous chapters. The unpacking and understanding of the standards and the creation of assessments and tasks that support learning are critical to create a classroom environment with the focus on learning. Teachers have to clearly define, for themselves and the students, what the expected outcome is for the learning. They have to create formative assessments that match the progression of the expected outcome. Those formative assessments will lead to the differentiation. As was modeled in chapter 6, students will get different work and support with the learning when they indicate they have a gap in understanding. Not everyone needs the same thing. Some will be moved beyond and challenged, while others will need the support to build the understanding. What the student needs, the teacher will provide.

I always liken this to taking a trip. I used to tell my students at the beginning of the year that we were taking a learning trip. If we were taking a trip to New York, we might not all choose the same route. We will take the route that is right for us, but we will all be at our destination at the end of the year. That is what differentiation is about. All of the students have the grade-level standards as the goal because that is the ultimate destination. Many will need an alternate route to get there, but they will get there because the teacher will differentiate the learning based upon their needs. The teacher will help them overcome the obstacles by making the learning applicable to the needs of the student.

In moving forward, it is important to talk about the difference between readiness and ability. Ability is viewed through one of the aforementioned mind-sets. Readiness relates to the previous learning of the student. If children come to the 3rd grade without automaticity of multiplication facts, they are less likely to be successful with multiple-digit multiplication. They lack a skill that will make the process easier. That is not to say they cannot be successful, but it will require more work on their part and that may impact the success. We all learn those pesky facts at different rates. A student without automaticity will need supports to move to the more complicated level of the skill. That would be considered differentiation. You might provide a chart when they are working with multiplication problems. They can be engaged with the grade-level task with a support that allows them to not be overwhelmed by the process. The repetitive use of the chart might help them to memorize some of the facts as well. Some critics might say that it is not fair that one child gets the chart and others don't. I have to say, I hear that from teachers more than students. The students seem to understand that some of their classmates need support and others don't. I happen to be five foot three. If I need to get something out of a cupboard, I might need a footstool. Someone who is not vertically challenged will not need that help. Should I not get the footstool because they don't need one? It is an issue of equity, not equality. In a classroom, everyone should get what they need. That is equity, and it requires differentiation.

Differentiation can be based on readiness (precursor knowledge), student interest (to get them engaged), or learning profile (modalities and learning issues) (Sousa & Tomlinson, 2011). It is not complicated. The focus here is on simple classroom changes that address the ideas of differentiation. When thinking about differentiating for a student, the following three areas should be considered: content, process, and product. These three areas should form the structure for differentiation in the classroom. Let's take a look at each one closely.

CONTENT

Content is analogous to curriculum. It is what is being taught. Everything that a teacher uses to teach a subject is related to the content. However, when thinking about the information, access should be first and foremost in the mind of the teacher. In order to develop an understanding, students need to be able to access the information in a way that allows them to build connections between new learning and previous learning. Differentiation of content is never about dumbing down the information; it is about making the information comprehensible to the student. The following are questions to guide content differentiation:

- Can all of the students in my class access the material and the learning?
- What might be interfering with the access? (language acquisition, readiness)
- How can that be remedied so that they can learn the material and meet the objective?

There are a variety of reasons that students might not be able to fully access the information a teacher has prepared. The most obvious might be that their reading level is keeping them from comprehending the material written at grade level. That could be due to a variety of factors, but, in any case, must be addressed by the teacher. Oftentimes a teacher can access information from a source in the textbook that presents the information with simpler text. Making sure that students have access to that reading would be an effective differentiation for them. Another content differentiation might be having the students listen to the content rather than read it. Again, most textbooks have an audio component, so the teacher has access to this easily. Students might be able to understand it when it is read to them but cannot actually do the reading.

Students might not be able to fully access the material because of a language barrier. English learners will, most likely, not have the content vocabulary in English. A teacher might have to frontload the content vocabulary in a way that provides them with a visual support to fully understand the word. While this can be done with the whole class, it might be done in a small group prior to the reading, which would allow them to more fully comprehend the material. There also might be reading material in their native language that would enable them to understand the content at a higher level as well. There is no "one size fits all" approach. Teachers who know the students are the best ones to determine the most effective differentiation for content support.

Modalities also play a role in students developing an understanding. While some students do well with reading or listening to a lecture, others do not. A student who needs visuals might benefit from a pictorial input chart where content is supported with pictures. This is a teaching strategy that works well with English learners and visual learners. Examples of such

charts can be accessed using the following link: http://www.bing.com/im-
ages/search?q=pictorial+input+charts&qpvt=pictoral+input+charts.

You will see that the charts are rich with language that will support the
learning of content for English learners. This strategy is one from the Project
GLAD program (Guided Language Acquisition Design). It is one way of
differentiating content.

Another strategy used by GLAD is the addition of music for learning.
Creating songs that are content rich and sung repetitively throughout a unit
helps those learners who need the support to learn the content. A song is
remembered for a long time. I can still sing content songs I learned 40 years
ago. It is a powerful tool. Adding motions to the song enables kinesthetic
learners to have more access to the content. Students are engaged in singing
or chanting and physical movement to cement learning.

For instance, as a part of a unit on animals, I may want the students to
fully understand the following vocabulary terms: *carnivore, omnivore, herbi-
vore, consumer,* and *producer.* Creating a chant could help with that.

> **What I Eat (sung to "Twinkle Twinkle Little Star")**
> Animals don't eat the same
> What they eat determines the name
> Meat eaters are carnivores
> Lions, tigers, and some more
> Omnivores they eat it all
> Plants and meat make up their diet
> Herbivores just like the plants
> Elephants also giraffes
> Now you know the names my friend
> Sing this song to remember them

While singing this song, you could add a motion that will help students
remember the differences. For instance, for omnivores you could have them
point to themselves. When singing about carnivores they could pantomime a
lion. You get it. Make it fun, engaging, and memorable. They are getting
content in another way. Writing the song out on a chart will lead to further
discussion, and you could have them talk about the similarities and differences. Remember these are classified as highly effective strategies for learning by Marzano (2003). The chart could also serve as reading practice for
students. Another consideration would be to add visuals to the chart. This
would help students make more connections to the content as well. The
visuals could be cut out from a magazine or can be created by the teacher and

students. All of this makes the learning more comprehensible. So much in one little song!

Try It: Think of a subject that you might teach. Then think of at least five vocabulary words that you would want the students to remember. Choose a familiar tune and be creative. Share your work with a few people, and they can share theirs. Now you have several content songs to use.

Student interest can be taken into account with the choice of material the class will be engaged with during the unit. Why do all students have to study the same animals? Students can have choice about what animal they are researching. Teachers simply have to have a wide variety of books available and students get to choose. For instance, when learning about herbivores you might choose to have books and zoo magazines with a variety of animals. You might also have a station that utilizes an online source for information. Students can access the information in the ways that are best for them. It is not limited to the textbook. I would even search out animals that students might not think of right away. By including slugs, green iguanas, or a giant tortoise, you might spark the interest of the students to explore the topic in more depth.

PROCESS

Process is about the students' metacognition. This is what is going on in their heads to make sense of the learning. This is where they might compare new information to known information in order to understand the content in a new or deeper way. Students do not all process information in the same way (Sousa & Tomlinson, 2011). It is best to utilize a variety of learning opportunities that allow students to process information. Just like the content, readiness, interest, and learning styles should be taken into account. Some guiding questions for you here might be:

- What support might the students need to see the connections? (graphic organizers, color coding)
- How will I provide help for those with language needs?
- What scaffolds will help students who are not ready for the independent work?

The process can be scaffolded for readiness or learning profile in a variety of ways. You can increase or decrease complexity. For instance, if you are asking students to compare and contrast herbivores, carnivores, and omnivores some might be ready to do all three together using a complex Venn diagram. Others might need to only do two at a time. Some might need an alternate organizer to make sense of the comparison. Partner work might be a scaffold for some students. Strategic partners can be assigned by the teacher to support the learning. In the case of an English learner, a native speaker might be a good partner. If students need support in their first language, it can be given. Students might also need a word bank or sentence frames if they do not have the necessary language or writing skills.

Another differentiation might be allowing the students choice in working. Some students prefer a quiet workplace, and others prefer working in groups. Give them choice about how they work. This choice relates to their learning profile. Making sure that there are quiet work zones in the classroom is essential for some learners. Study carrels work well for this. It is one way that students can limit distractions. I have also used headphones for some students. This allows them to work in a quiet environment within the classroom when others are working in groups. Some students process information verbally. I have worked with many who simply need to speak about it before they see the connections. They can solve their problems, but they need to process out loud. They can be working with a partner or a small group. They could even be allowed to process with the teacher at a specific time. Not providing avenues for students to process information in different ways leaves some out of the understanding. One caveat for this type of learning is that you must have good class management skills. Students have to know what work looks like; there must be accountability and structure, which must be put into place at the beginning of the year. If the students are not working effectively, they might lose the opportunity. I have seen, for the most part, that students like this so they make sure they are on task and finish.

The process can be altered for interest as well. Students can choose the animal from the group they would like to compare. Why does everyone have to do the same two? If groups and individuals get to choose, you have more examples. Students can then share with one another, and the learning deepens. The sharing can be with the whole class or in a small group; it is dependent upon the time available. Now instead of only comparing two animals, they have participated in several examples, and the concept of comparing and contrasting is clearer to them. They can even be challenged to critique or add to the work of another group. The possibilities are endless, really.

PRODUCT

Products can be equated to summative assessments. They are the culminating activity for the unit. It is how the students will demonstrate their full understanding of the topic and the standards. In my day, when we were studying animals, we all had to write a report at the end. The report had a certain format, and all students used that format. I can only imagine how boring it was for the teacher to read. It was equally boring for the students to write. Why does everyone have to present the information in the same way? Don't we want to allow students to have some creativity? Here are some guiding questions to consider:

- What should the students include to demonstrate full understanding? (This comes from unpacking the standard.)
- What are the possible ways that students could demonstrate understanding? (report, presentation, web-based option)
- What is the best way to evaluate the options I give? (rubrics, scoring guides, assessment)
- Does understanding have to be demonstrated individually? (A group presentation might be okay.)

I challenge you to open your mind about how students can express their understanding. Be open to allowing a variety of products at the end of a unit. Some students might not have the writing skills to pull off a report. If I am concerned with content, I could allow them to do a PowerPoint presentation instead. They will be demonstrating oral language skills rather than writing skills. I would simply adjust the rubric to grade the oral language. This would require less writing on their part, but it is not less rigorous. The elements that are important parts of the standards have to be there, but the product is different. This can also be used for book reports. Students can report on a book by presenting something rather than writing. I would still be able to gauge their comprehension and their understanding of the story elements because the structure for the report would clearly indicate what must be included and at what depth.

Student interest is immediately addressed when there is choice in the product. Students can choose to do something that they find interesting (Sousa & Tomlinson, 2011). The guidelines have to be clear and the criteria rigorous so that they are meaningful products. Many will do a mediocre job on a report but become wildly creative if they are allowed to present something in a poster. For instance, when I taught habitats in my 4th-grade class, my students were allowed choice in the product. Some produced murals and explained them in a presentation. Others wrote a report or created a brochure that might be used by visitors to the zoo. They all demonstrated their understanding of the elements of a habitat, a food web, and the other criteria necessary. They simply presented the knowledge in a different way.

Group projects can be used as a final assessment if they are structured correctly. During the process of creating the product, teachers need to be conscious of interacting with students to determine their individual understanding. Every student must have an active role in the presentation. A group project format allows for the teacher to provide lots of feedback during the process, and every interaction is a formative assessment. That interaction would include the open-ended questions discussed earlier. The teacher is learning something about the students and their understanding. Sometimes the teacher does not need to engage, he or she just has to listen to the interaction. Instead, the teacher could use the time to record anecdotal notes about the understanding.

One great option for a group project is inviting parents and others in for the presentations. There was a lot of excitement in my classroom on presentation days. It was celebrated. One person I always invited was the principal. He or she was always amazed at the knowledge and the presentation skills of the students. The parents and the principal were also impressed at what I could tell them about the students when we sat down for a conversation. Those anecdotal notes supported all I had to say about students. It made conferences with parents and my principal much easier. Parents feel comforted when the teacher can express a true understanding of their child.

If the product is a test, you can also vary that. Why does everyone have to take the exact same test? The format might be changed based on the needs of the students. Why can't students express their understanding to the teacher orally? Ask the questions in a way that allows students to present their understanding in a variety of ways. When crafting the directions for an essay question, consider the following phrase: Using words and/or pictures explain _____. Students might be asked to explain photosynthesis, the main message of a story, or how to solve a math problem. If they do not possess the language to do that in writing, they can support their answer with a diagram or a picture. The important thing is that the teacher is able to see what the students understand and what they don't. That is the point of an assessment. Not all students will be able to effectively demonstrate that in the same manner.

Right now you are probably thinking that I am crazy and this will take too much work. Well, testing with an essay question that allows different forms of expression rather than some selected response questions may take a little more time to grade, but it will be worth it when you see the learning. That simple differentiation will work for most students. The students who might need to tell you what they know will be very low in number. That is a rare differentiation. If your goal is students' success, why not give them the best chance for success? That is at the core of this work. Being a great teacher is hard work; no one said it would be easy.

The process of thinking about differentiation in a classroom has to begin with a brainstorming session. What are some of the possibilities? Getting ideas down will help open ways of thinking about what you will include in the learning throughout the unit. One way to organize that is in a table. At a grade-level meeting, open the discussion and accept all ideas. The process of thinking about teaching in this way will help shift the paradigm and enable all to see the possibilities for rich, meaningful experiences for the learners.

Here are some ideas for planning a persuasive writing unit. You will see there are ideas about how to provide alternatives for all learners in the three areas.

Content

- Varied examples at different reading and writing levels
- Include speeches (YouTube, etc.) to help students see the reason for persuasion
- Create supportive charts for the steps and criteria for the letter
- Student-friendly rubric

Process

- Allow partners to create a persuasive paper or speech
- Provide specific organizers that allow the development of portions of the product
- Small-group instruction with teacher to guide
- Different requirements for feedback checks—some whole letter, some portions at due dates

- Increase complexity by having students prepare arguments from an alternate point of view

Product

- Student chooses topic and audience
- Teacher provides topic and audience
- Letter, presentation with notes, poster, video, panel discussion
- Students can also choose to present out of school (school board meeting, etc.)

Now the team will be able to go about finding those examples of persuasive writing at various levels of reading ability. The rubrics and the graphic organizers will need to be developed. The criteria for the alternate projects at the end would need to be determined as well. The individual tasks can be distributed to the team members and brought back to be shared among the team. The old adage "many hands make light work" applies here. Now, more than ever, we need to take a collaborative approach to planning and teaching. This is complex work and cannot be as effectively done in isolation. It also models collaboration for students. If we want students to work together, they should see teachers working together.

Try It: Work together in a group of three or four. Choose a topic for a unit of study. A few examples might be the solar system, fractions and decimals, friendly letter writing, or the American Revolution. How might you differentiate for content, process, and product? Present your ideas to another group or the whole class or staff. How did this help you think about the process?

Content: How will you provide access to content?

Process: How will you help students through the learning?

Product: What will demonstrate that they have learned the content? How will you assess it?

Chapter Eight

Feedback for Learning

We are nearing the end here. So far, we have looked at what assessment is, how it should be structured and planned, the writing of the items, the alignment to the standards, the analysis of results for planned action, the choosing of strategies, and the differentiation in the classroom. Now, let's talk specifically about how to help the students take more control of the learning. We are, after all, trying to help students become independent and self-directed learners. The right assessment piece, as we previously learned, helps the teacher determine the problems in understanding. The right feedback helps the students begin to correct the problems. The formative, standards-based assessments that are planned throughout a unit will give multiple opportunities for feedback that will increase performance and achievement.

What is feedback? We have all gotten a paper returned to us with "Good Job," "Excellent," or "Fantastic" written across the top. What part of the paper was excellent or fantastic? What did I do that was so great? Those kinds of comments are praise, not feedback. According to Wiggins (2012), "feedback is information about how we are doing in our efforts to reach a goal." Feedback is not advice; it is specific and goal referenced. For our purposes, it must be tied directly to the standards as well. It must be clear so the recipient will be able to take action upon it to come closer to achieving the standard. Feedback must also be ongoing and consistent in order to guide the learning. Think back on the learning loop. Feedback is given when the agreed upon strategies are employed in individual classrooms. During that time, students work and receive targeted feedback, which is how the learning is guided. It must occur during the learning so there is time for the students to act upon it (Chappuis, 2012). The goal has been clearly defined by the team, and all of the feedback given to students will be focused and tightly aligned to the standards that define the goal.

There are many ways to deliver feedback to a student. It really is dependent on the assignment. For instance, written feedback is often used when providing feedback on a writing process. Oral feedback, given during a work session, works well when providing guidance when solving math problems or constructing a sentence. It also works well when guiding group tasks. This will take a bit of practice. Many times teachers simply provide an answer here, but that will not help the student. For instance, when a student has made a multiplication error, the teacher might say "4 times 5 is 20, not 25." That is not feedback; the teacher is doing the thinking. Instead, tell the student that there is a multiplication error and have him or her go about finding and changing it. Oral feedback allows a teacher to take advantage of those "teachable moments" to further student understanding. Just like written feedback, it must be aligned to the standards.

Another form of feedback is modeling or demonstrations. This is used in a variety of ways. When a student is holding a pencil incorrectly and a teacher models the correct way, they are enabling the student to change by demonstrating the correct technique (Brookhart, 2008). There are times when a model serves best for learning. Students can follow along, and feedback can be given as they develop the skill.

When deciding what feedback is appropriate for the student, a teacher must take many variables into account. They need to think about the developmental level of the student, the language proficiency, the reading ability, and the emotional needs of the student. If a student is not able to read the written feedback or comprehend it, it will not be effective. For that student, verbal feedback would be best. Feedback that is beyond the ability of the student to correct will not be able to be acted upon. Not every student will react to feedback in the same way. Teachers must get to know their students and what they can handle. The ultimate goal is for the students to act upon the feedback. By knowing the readiness of the students and what they are able to handle, the right amount and type of feedback can be provided.

Written feedback is generally provided right on the work. It can be done using a rubric, but notes should accompany the selection of the rubric grade so the students know exactly what is done well and what might be lacking in relation to the standards included in the task. The feedback provided by the teacher must be tied closely to the goal and clear to the students. The teacher must be clear about the goal but so must the students. As Chappuis (2012) notes, "absent a learning target, students will believe that the goal is to complete the activity." We really want the students to be focused on learning rather than simply completing the assignment. For instance, the goal of a persuasive writing piece is to do just that, persuade someone to do something we want. So if I am providing feedback to a student about this type of writing, I need to remain focused on the goal of persuading the reader. The standard requires the language choice to be convincing. I cannot simply say "this is not convincing"; I must be clear about what is not convincing. By being too vague, I run the risk of the student not understanding and being able to take the feedback and put it to use. I must be clear about why the writing was not convincing to me as the reader. Here is an example of written feedback to consider:

Remember that you are trying to choose persuasive points that are meaningful to the reader because you want to convince them to agree with you. Would this be meaningful to them or you? What might make it more meaningful to the reader? What would be important to them? What might their arguments be about this issue?

The questions given to the student are directly related to the goal of the paper. They are meant to guide the thinking about the revision. This would be best done in a conference so the teacher can hear the student verbally process her ideas and then guide the student's thinking if necessary. It is all about clarifying. Some students will need more support than others. I caution against writing it for the student. The goal is to help the student create the argument. If you write examples, it is just like providing the answer to a math problem. The thinking stops because the solution is there. Help the student find a solution rather than select one for them.

One area that is particularly vulnerable for solving rather than guiding in written feedback is when a teacher is providing convention corrections. In any writing unit, the standards regarding conventions play a role. Rather than providing the correct solution, employ a coding system so the students know there is a problem, but they have to determine it and fix it. For this kind of feedback, a simple letter system would work. For instance, you might use a C for some kind of capitalization error, an S for spelling, and a G for grammar. Initially you may indicate the problem by putting the letter right at the spot of the error. The placement of the correction would change as the year progresses to the beginning of the line. This would require that the students look at the whole line and determine the error. To further expand this, you might evolve to a tally system at the top of the page or paragraph telling how many errors were seen. This is an example of the gradual release of responsibility that Fisher and Frey (2008) advocate for in their structure for teaching and learning. The goal is independence as a writer; the teacher's actions must promote that independence. For example:

(C, S, G, C) Chrishper clumbus had three ships. The names of the ship were nina, pinta, and santa maria.

I have alerted the student that there are capitalization, spelling, and grammar errors in the sentence. It is up to the student to locate them and fix them. The student will need to use supportive materials to get the spelling correct. It is important that the student does it rather than the teacher. If each error is corrected by the teacher, it results in too much feedback, and the student will rely too heavily upon it. As the time progresses, I might give the following feedback instead. For example:

(* * * * * * * *) Chrishper clumbus had three ships. The names of the ship were nina, pinta, and santa maria.

The dot system allows the teacher to communicate the number of errors in the sentence, but the students themselves have to determine the kind of error. More thinking on the part of the student is required for this kind of support. The level of support would be determined by the needs of the student.

If oral feedback was given to the student in the above example, a teacher might simply tell the student to remember the rules for proper nouns. That gives a clue as to what to attend to, but the student alone has to identify which are the proper nouns.

Feedback is something that is ongoing and consistent. Think of a coach here. There is a lot of feedback on stance, swing, and follow-through for a batter before a game is played. There are drills specifically designed to help with all of the elements involved. The batter gets better as he or she practices. The activities and the assignments planned as part of a unit are the opportunities for practice of the elements of whatever is being taught, and the students need the corrective feedback in order to be able to perform at the optimum when needed. Feedback on strengths and errors will help the students to build resilience. Helping them to see where they are strong gives them a feeling of success. Delivering the error correction in a way that demonstrates a belief that they are capable of the next step will help them to persevere in the task. This takes time and requires the creation of a trusting relationship between the teacher and the students. When the paradigm around classwork shifts from completion of tasks to demonstration of learning, students' anxiety goes down. They see the work as an opportunity for growth rather than a judgment. They know they will receive positive and corrective feedback so they can improve. They also know their teacher believes they will have success in the learning.

One important caveat to the feedback loop is this: when students demonstrate they do not have even a partial understanding of the concept, feedback is not effective. When the student's work demonstrates little or no understanding of the concepts or steps necessary for completion, it is best addressed by reteaching (Hattie & Timperley, 2007). Corrective feedback builds on learning. If the student did not learn the concept or skill, feedback will not help to move the understanding forward. Hattie and Timperley (2007) note that, in this case, the corrective feedback can have a negative emotional effect. That will certainly interfere with the resilience mentioned earlier. Students need to know they will get what they need. That might be feedback, or it might be a new lesson with a different approach. The different approach will send a message to the students that there is a belief that they will gain understanding and there is a willingness to work with them to do that. How will you know when something should be retaught? Chappuis (2012) suggests that when there is no legitimate positive feedback that can be given tied to the specific skill, it is a sign that you should, more than likely, reteach the lesson.

Feedback given to a student should always be a mix of support and affirmation. Students are doing something right. Acknowledge the partial understandings or the successes and then move to some corrective feedback. Many of us have bad memories of receiving a paper back from a teacher full of red ink. Every error we made was highlighted, and it might have been overwhelming. That approach will shut students down. Chances are they will feel that there is too much to tackle. Choose a reasonable amount of correction for a student; the amount to offer is certainly impacted by the individual student. Some are able to handle more than others. The goal is to move the learning forward. Concentrate on errors that, if fixed, would move the work forward.

Going back to the previous example of a persuasive writing piece, it might mean simply concentrating on one paragraph for feedback and not the aper. Since the introduction is where you state the position, it would ˍ ˍ gical place to begin. Students may need help with a portion of that, and the rest of the paper will be left until later. It is a way of chunking the work so the student does not get discouraged. Many reluctant writers will shut down if they have to rewrite the whole paper. If it is framed to only work on the first paragraph and a few sentences within it, the student is likely to complete the work without becoming discouraged. It is manageable and probably will not result in a shut down or a refusal to work. Now, because there is differentiation, other students might be working on more of the writing. That is expected. Feedback, like the work, needs to be differentiated for students so that it results in change.

Another important consideration about any feedback is the tone. That is a consideration in both oral and written feedback. Think about how the message will be received. That again is dependent upon the student and the variables mentioned earlier. The tone impacts how the message will be "heard" (Brookhart, 2008). If you plan to tell a student what is wrong, provide guidance on fixing the problem in a way that makes the student take an active role in remedying it. Sarcasm, which can easily be interpreted as degrading the student, does not belong in feedback. That will not help build the relationship that will support learning.

When providing feedback, it is best to use descriptive language tied to the criteria of the assignment. For instance, when providing feedback on a persuasive piece of writing, saying "good word choice" is vague. However, "your use of figurative language here is a good tool for helping your reader see your position" is more descriptive and tells the student what was good about the word choice and how it relates to the standard.

Along with tone, choosing when and where to provide the feedback is an important consideration. Sometimes a private conversation is needed for delivering feedback. For oral feedback, a student can come to the teacher's desk. It could also be quietly provided at the student's desk. It can be given extemporaneously or planned as a part of a conference. When addressing a group, I have found it best to actually sit down with the group and become involved in the discussions. By sitting, it helps students see that the teacher is joining the group and bringing support for the work. It also sends the message that there is a belief that the group can succeed with the task. The growth mind-set is in action here (Dweck, 2006).

Many teachers use peer feedback structures as well. This allows students to provide feedback to one another. Peer feedback helps students because it helps them develop a clearer understanding of the standard-based criteria involved in the learning. When they are able to evaluate other people's work, it can make them better at evaluating their own work. They also get to see alternate approaches to the task. That is helpful because there is not only one way to approach a task. This could help the development of "out of the box" thinking. There are challenges with this kind of feedback. First of all, it is not generally as specific and targeted. This can be helped with a targeted form, but students are not experts in the task. They can give helpful feedback from a reader's standpoint, but the teacher is in the best position to give truly effective feedback.

Students need help knowing how to use the feedback provided on assignments. It is not natural for a student to apply feedback. The classroom must be set up in a way that feedback is acted upon and then reevaluated. The loop is a constant. If the student is simply working on one paragraph, as suggested earlier, then at the end of the work session the paragraph is resubmitted. This is the formative assessment loop, and the feedback will drive next steps until the product is complete. If the student did not engage in changing the work, then the new feedback might be on task completion. The expectation is that the work will be done and improved. The expectations are high, and the work is fully supported. That is the way to help students grow.

Remember that feedback is a part of the assessment process. It is a way to help students see what they are doing well and what they can improve. It is a way to guide the understanding and move students along in their learning. It does not matter if the feedback is written, oral, or a demonstration of a technique; the student must be able to understand and act upon it to make it effective for learning. As long as it is clear, focused, and aligned to the purpose of the task, it will result in success for the learner. That is what we all want.

Try It: Your 5th-grade student has produced the writing sample, shown in figure 8.1. He is an English learner who has been in the country for one year. His CELDT (California English Language Development Test) result is a 3. Here is a descriptor of that level:

Intermediate—Students performing at this level of English-language proficiency begin to tailor their English-language skills to meet communication and learning demands with increasing accuracy. They are able to identify and understand more concrete details and some major abstract concepts during unmodified instruction. They are able to respond with increasing ease to more varied communication and learning demands with a reduced number of errors. Oral and written production has usually expanded to sentences, para-graphs, and original statements and questions. Errors still complicate com-munication   (web.stanford.edu/~hakuta/Courses/Ed388   Website/Assign-ments).

Here are the guiding standards for the paper. You can employ a persua-sive writing rubric of your choosing to provide targeted feedback. What feedback would you provide? What needs to be attended to first? Where are they succeeding in relation to the standards? Where are they struggling? How would you go about delivering the feedback?

CCSS.ELA-Literacy.W.5.1.a

Introduce a topic or text clearly, state an opinion, and create an organiza-tional structure in which ideas are logically grouped to support the writer's purpose.

CCSS.ELA-Literacy.W.5.1.b

Provide logically ordered reasons that are supported by facts and details.

CCSS.ELA-Literacy.W.5.1.c

Link opinion and reasons using words, phrases, and clauses (e.g., *consequently, specifically*).

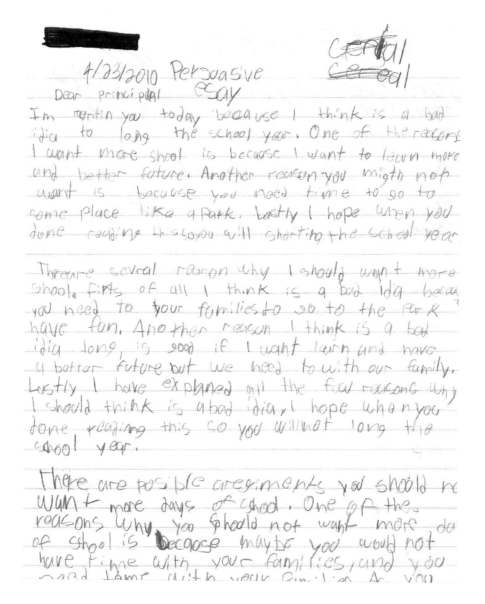

Figure 8.1. 5th-Grade Writing Sample.

References

Ainsworth, L. (2003a). *Power standards: Identifying the standards that matter most.* Englewood, CO: Lead and Learn Press.

Ainsworth, L. (2003b). *Unwrapping the standards: A simple process to make standards manageable.* Englewood, CO: The Leadership and Learning Center.

Ainsworth, L., Kamm, C., Peery, A., Pitchford, B., & Rose, A. (2011). *Common formative assessments* (2nd ed.). Englewood, CO: The Leadership and Learning Center.

Ainsworth, L., & Viegut, D. (2006). *Common formative assessments: How to connect standards-based instruction and assessment.* Thousand Oaks, CA: Corwin.

Brookhart, S. (2008). *How to give effective feedback to your students.* Alexandria, VA: ASCD.

Brookhart, S. (2013). *How to create and use rubrics.* Alexandria, VA: ASCD.

Chappuis, J. (2012, September). How am I doing? *Educational Leadership, 70*(1), 36–40.

Covey, S. (1989). *The seven habits of highly effective people: Powerful lessons in personal change.* New York: Free Press.

Datnow, A., Park, V., & Wohlstetter, P. (2007). Achieving with data: How high-performing elementary systems use data to improve student achievement. Los Angeles: Center for Educational Governance, University of Southern California.

Dial, E. (2011). Exploring pathways for school improvement and the development of high reliability through qeia funding. Dissertation. University of California, San Diego.

Dial, E. (2015). Creating confident, effective teachers by changing pre-service programs to promote resilience, assessment literacy, and collaboration. *National Teacher Education Journal, 8*(1), 33–39.

Doran, G. T. (1981). There's a S.M.A.R.T. way to write management's goals and objectives. Management Review, 70, 35–36.

Dweck, C. S. (2006). *Mindset: The new psychology of success.* New York: Random House.

Fisher, D., & Frey, N. (2008). *Better learning through structured teaching: A framework for the gradual release of responsibility.* Alexandria, VA: ASCD.

Hattie, J. A. (1992). Measuring the effects of schooling. *Australian Journal of Education, 36*(1), 5–13.

Hattie, J. A., & Timperley, H. (2007). The power of feedback. *Review of Educational Research, 77*(1), 81–112.

Kagan, S. (1994). *Cooperative learning.* San Clemente, CA: Kagan Publishing.

Kagan, S., & Kagan, M. (2009). *Kagan cooperative learning*. San Clemente, CA: Kagan Publishing.

Marzano, R. (2003). *What works in schools: Translating research into action*. Alexandria, VA: ASCD.

Popham, J. (2003). *Test better, teach better: The instructional role of assessment*. Alexandria, VA: ASCD.

Popham, W. J. (1999). Where large-scale assessment is heading and why it shouldn't. *Educational Measurement: Issues and Practice, 18*(3), 13–17.

Shepard, L. A. (2001). The role of classroom assessment in teaching and learning. In V. Richardson (Ed.), *Handbook of research on teaching* (4th ed., 1066–1101). Washington, DC: AERA.

Sousa, D., & Tomlinson, C. (2011). *Differentiation and the brain: How neuroscience supports the learner-friendly classroom*. Bloomington, IN: Solution Tree Press.

Spillane, J. (2006). *Distributed leadership*. San Francisco, CA: Jossey Bass.

Stiggins, R., & Chappuis, J. (12/01/2006). What a difference a word makes. *Journal of Staff Development, 27*(1), 10–14.

Stiggins, R. J. (1997). *Student-centered classroom assessment* (2nd ed.). Columbus, Ohio: Merrill.

Wiggins, G. (2012). 7 keys to effective feedback. *Educational Leadership, 70*(1), 10–16.

Wiggins, G., & McTighe, J. (2005). *Understanding by Design (Expanded 2nd ed.)*. Alexandria, VA: ASCD.

Yorke, M. (2003). Formative assessment in higher education: Moves towards theory and the enhancement of pedagogic practice. *Higher Education, 45*, 477–501.

Index

above level for learning, 43, 92–94
accommodations, 45
affirmation, 111
Ainsworth, Larry, 21, 22–23, 52, 65, 66, 79
analysis of results, 75, 92–94
analytic rubrics, 60
anecdotal notes, 10
Annenberg Institute for School Reform, 82
assessment. *See* formative assessment;
    summative assessment
assessment format, 51, 63. *See also*
    constructed response questions; rubrics;
    selected response questions
assessment instrument validity, 16–18, 17
assessment of readiness, 92

Backward Design, 38
basic level of learning, 92–94
below level of learning, 45, 92–94
binary choice, 54–55, 73, 76
Bloom's Taxonomy, 66, 67, 68
brainstorming sessions, 105–106

calendar for planning, 30
Chappuis, J., 108, 111
chunks of work, 29, 33, 112
classroom interventions, 2
closed questions, 11, 12
coach analogy, 110
collaboration, 63, 71, 82–83, 105–106

comparing and contrasting strategy, 85,
    102
constructed response questions: extended
    response, 58–59, 60, 61, 62; rubrics, 58,
    59, 60, 61, 62; short answer, 57, 59;
    uses, 75
construct validity, 16, 17
content, focus on, 21–25
content differentiation, 98–101, 105
content validity, 17, 18
convention corrections, 109
cooperative learning tasks, 87
Covey, Stephen, 38
criterion validity, 16, 17
curriculum. *See* content differentiation

decision making. *See* TIDES Learning
    Loop
demonstration as feedback, 108
desirable standards, 25
differentiation: about, 95; accommodations
    and modifications, 45; content, 98–101,
    105; focus on, 97–98; IEP, 45; lesson
    design for, 37, 43–45; mind-set and,
    95–97; partner teams, 46; planning for,
    26, 28, 32; process, 101–102, 105–106;
    product, 103–105, 106; Try It exercises,
    101, 106
discussions as formative assessment, 10
Dweck, Carol, 95

119

effect size, 85
effort reinforcement, 86
endurance of standards, 22–23
English learners: feedback to, 113–114,
    115; lesson plans for, 6–7, 37, 45,
    99–100; verbal summaries used by, 86
enrichment tasks, 43
essential standards, 22–23, 28, 38. *See also*
    formative assessments
exit tickets, 11
extended response questions, 58–59, 60,
    61, 62

feedback to students: affirmation and, 111;
    coach analogy, 110; defined, 107;
    delivery of, 42, 46, 108–110, 112;
    examples, 109, 110; from peers, 112;
    reteaching instead of, 111; rubrics used
    for 87; students applying, 113; tone of,
    69, 112; Try It exercises, 113–114, 115.
    See also formative assessment
fill-in-the-blank questions, 56, 74, 77
final exams, 14
Fisher, D., 109
fixed mind-set, 95–96
focus standards, 28, 33
formative assessments: collaboration and,
    71; effectiveness measured with, 5;
    goals, 4, 13; misconceptions with, 5–7;
    planning and, 26, 28; student readiness
    measured with, 7–9; summative
    assessment comparison, 4; Try It
    suggestions, 74–77, 77; types, 9–13;
    uses, 65, 74; validity of, 18. *See also*
    assessment format
Frey, N., 109

general rubrics, 60
GLAD (Guided Language Acquisition
    Design) Project, 100
goals in lesson design, 38–42
grade-level teams, 75, 88, 105–106. *See
    also* TIDES Learning Loop
graphic organizers, 32, 42, 69, 85
group work for students, 102, 104, 112
growth mind-set, 95, 112
Guided Language Acquisition Design
    (GLAD) Project, 100
guided practice format, 42

Hattie, J. A., 85, 111
highly desirable standards, 23–24, 38
holistic rubrics, 60
homework, 86
hypothesis testing, 87

I Do, We Do, You Do structure, 32
Individualized Education Plan (IEP), 45
inferences about learning, 83–84
informal rubrics, 61, 62
instructional practices, 82–83, 85–87
interventions, 2, 88

Jot Thoughts, 12–13

Kagan, M., 10, 12
Kagan, S., 10, 12

language barriers, 99–100. *See also*
    English learners
learning loop. *See* TIDES Learning Loop
lesson design: assessment and, 46; closure,
    46; defined, 37; differentiation, 37,
    43–45; objectives, 38–42; planning
    process affecting, 38; pretests, 8–9, 40;
    procedures/teaching, 42; reflection,
    46–48; samples, 39–40, 47; template,
    38, 39–40, 49; Try It suggestions, 48
leverage of standards, 23
lifelong learning encouragement, 96

MAPS (Measures of Academic Progress),
    81
Marzano, R., 85, 87, 95
matching items, 55–56, 73, 76
math examples, 5–7, 66–70, 70
McTighe, J., 38
Measures of Academic Progress (MAPS),
    81
measures of effectiveness, 5
metacognition, 101
mind-sets, 95–96, 112
modalities, 99–100
modeling as feedback, 108
model thinking, 42, 45
modifications, 45
multiple choice, 53–54, 72, 72–73, 76
Murdoch, Rosario, 90–92
music for learning, 100

nonlinguistic representation, 87
note taking, 86
Numbered Heads, 10

objectives in lesson design, 38–42
Oliveri, Stephanie, 90–92
one-on-one interventions, 2
on level, procedures for, 44
open questions, 11–12, 33, 104

pacing guides, 27, 34
partner talk structure, 42, 44
partner teams, 46
pedagogy decisions, 28–29, 65, 70, 95
peer feedback, 112
peer tutors, 9, 43
pie graph, 72, 74
planning process: beginning with end in
    mind, 38; calendar for, 30; focus on
    content, 21–25; importance of, 21, 34,
    90; long-term, 25, 27–29; need for
    explicitness in, 37; short-term, 25–26;
    Try It suggestions, 25, 34. *See also*
    lesson design; writing instruction
Popham, James, 15, 21, 23, 55
posttests, 9
practice with homework, 86
praise, 107
presentations as student option, 103, 104
pretests, 8–9, 40
procedures/teaching, 42
process differentiation, 101–102, 105–106
product differentiation, 103–105, 106
proficient level of learning, 83–84, 84, 85,
    92–94
Project GLAD (Guided Language
    Acquisition Design), 100

questions in formative assessment, 11–12

readiness: ability compared to, 97; criteria
    of standards, 23; formative assessment
    measuring, 7–9; importance of
    assessing, 92. *See also* differentiation
reading levels, 99
realia, 6
recall of information, 52
reflection, 26
reinforcement of student effort, 86

Response to Intervention (RtI) process,
    1–2, 3
reteaching, 111
revised informal rubrics, 62
road map analogy, 27
RtI (Response to Intervention) process,
    1–2, 3
rubrics: constructed response, 58, 59, 60,
    61, 62; developing, 61–63; math
    solution, 70; types, 60; uses, 41, 59

scaffolds for learning, 9, 101
selected response questions: about, 51–52;
    binary choice, 54–55, 73, 76;
    disadvantages of, 57; examples, 72,
    72–74; fill-in-the-blank questions, 56,
    74, 77; matching items, 55–56, 73, 76;
    multiple choice, 53–54; uses, 72, 75
sentence frames, 45
short answer questions, 57, 59
SMART goals, 88–90
Spillane, James, 71
standardized tests, 14–16, 16, 91
standards: feedback tied to, 107;
    identifying, 75; matching questions to,
    52; math content example, 66–70;
    rating, 22–25; unwrapping, 52, 65–66,
    67, 75. *See also* objectives in lesson
    design
state-mandated tests, 14–16, 16
students: group work, 102, 104, 112; mind-
    set, 96; reinforcing efforts of, 86. *See
    also* differentiation; feedback to
    students; readiness
summarization, 86
summative assessment: about, 13–16;
    formative assessment comparison, 4;
    products as, 103–105; validity of, 18.
    See also standardized tests; standards

task-specific rubrics, 60
teams. *See* TIDES Learning Loop
template for lesson design, 49
Test Better, Teach Better (Popham), 21
test format, 104–105
Think Aloud, 31–33, 42
Think-Pair-Share structure, 10, 65
TIDES Learning Loop: about, 80;
    collaboration of teachers on needs,

82–83; designing interventions, 85–88; drawing conclusions, 83–84, 84; initial compilation of results, 79–81, 81; SMART goals, 88–90; Try It suggestions, 89–90; uses, 79

Timperley, H., 111

validity of assessment instruments, 16–18, 17

verbal processing, 12

Viegut, D., 65

visuals for students, 6, 99, 100

white boards, 10–11

Wiggins, G., 38, 107

word banks, 45, 56

worksheet for RtI process, 3

writing instruction: Day 1, 31–32; Day 2, 33; graphic organizers, 32, 33, 34

Yorke, M., 71

About the Author

Eileen Dial is an associate professor at Holy Cross College in Notre Dame, Indiana. In addition to teaching courses in the field of education, she also serves as the director of student teaching and director of assessment at the college. Before coming to Holy Cross, she spent 16 years in the K–6 system as a teacher, a coach for new teachers, and a teacher leader. As a teacher leader, she was a part of three successful turnaround efforts in California. In her last position, she served as a data coach for teacher teams as they created and analyzed formative assessment as a part of a school turnaround effort.

In addition to the book *Assessment for Learning: A Practical Approach for the Classroom*, she has also published an article in the *National Teacher Education Journal* titled "An Experienced Practical Reflection: Creating Confident, Effective Teachers by Changing Pre-Service Programs to Promote Resilience, Assessment Literacy, and Collaboration." Dr. Dial has also presented at several conferences on the topic of assessment, and the topic continues to be the focus of her academic work.